Mike's latest book is a powerful narrative that showcases his profound impact in the project space. Having known him for years, I can attest to the authenticity of this work as a dynamic reflection of his expertise. Through compelling storytelling, Mike unpacks the fundamental principles of collaborative project delivery, providing readers with a roadmap to achieve success in their own projects.

**Mara Johnston | Managing Principal, Keystone**

Many organizations struggle to complete construction projects successfully. In *It's All About Your Team: One Team. Shared Success.*<sup>sm</sup> Michael Giaramita relies on his vast experience to create an excellent guide on how to achieve success. The insights he offers provide the key to delivering quality construction on schedule and within budget.

**Mark Burstein | President Emeritus, Lawrence University, former Executive Vice President at Princeton University**

Giaramita's insights underscore that effective team collaboration is not just about processes but is fundamentally about the relationships, trust, and shared commitment among team members.

**Bob Prieto | Chairman, Strategic Program Management LLC**

Giaramita's book is a must-read for anyone looking to master project delivery. His real-world case studies and practical strategies provide a blueprint for achieving extraordinary outcomes.

**Ibrahim Odeh | Founding Director, Global Leaders in Construction Management, Columbia University**

Michael Giaramita's *It's All About Your Team* is a masterclass in project management. His focus on collaboration and team alignment is truly transformative.

**Bob Accardi | RRA Consultant LLC, Former Executive Vice President at AECOM Tishman**

*It's All About Your Team* is a powerful exploration of the 'One Team, Shared Success.ˢᵐ' philosophy—a concept I've had the privilege of seeing in action firsthand. Having worked with Mike Giaramita on projects grounded in this approach, I can attest to its transformative impact on collaboration and results.

**Charles S. Maggio | Vice President, Turner & Townsend Healthcare**

# It's All About Your Team

## One Team. Shared Success.<sup>sm</sup>

Leaders Press

**MICHAEL GIARAMITA**

Leaders
Press

Front Cover Designer: Athena Longoria
Editor: Adelaide Godwin (Upspring)
Editor: Kathryn Harley (Upspring)
Editor: Lisa Gigliotti
Editor: Cara V. Lang

ISBN **978-1-63735-267-0** (pbk)
ISBN **978-1-63735-337-0** (hcv)
ISBN **978-1-63735-268-7** (ebook)

Library of Congress Control Number: 2024912778

# Foreword

Construction is easy in the abstract. It's like watching the conductor of an orchestra–it appears simple to coordinate scores of musicians and their instruments by merely moving your baton to the beat. That home renovation you have always contemplated must be a cakewalk…what could possibly go wrong? Surely, it cannot be that difficult and take so long to build the new airport we all so desperately need?

My foray into construction quickly took me from the abstract to reality. I was asked to step in and assume leadership of an occupied renovation of our headquarters building. The project was severely delayed and faced budget overruns. It required a reset, and the reasons were complex and multifaceted. I was a finance guy, new to construction, and I needed a guide–a wise and experienced mentor and most importantly, somebody without skin in the existing problems and challenges.

I am fortunate that Michael Giaramita became that mentor.

*It's All About Your Team* is Mike Giaramita's journey through four decades of working in construction. Mike has earned a well-deserved reputation as a *disruptor,* and nowhere is this more apparent than in his work on the Southwest Freeway in Texas (Chapter 2) where he proved the power of a proactive schedule and reduced a seven-year project to three. He excels at questioning the status quo and has the courage to try new approaches to age-old construction practices (Chapter 4).

In a world that is much bigger than just construction, the central theme of this accessible and readable book is that teams lie behind all of Mike's many achievements and indeed, any project's success. Several case studies (Chapters 3, 5, and 6), sprinkled with anecdotes and wisdom, illustrate his methods for aligning interests through culture change and building team spirit. *It's All About Your Team* provides home-spun advice and is a must-read for anybody involved in construction. If it works in a traditionally rigid and ego-driven industry, you can be sure it will also work elsewhere.

I was battling a discordant team when I first met Mike. Relationships were broken everywhere, not only within my own internal project team, but also with the general contractor, the trades, the architect, and even our advisory consultants. Everyone had different views on the diagnosis, but with one common thread: somebody else was to blame. I knew the project was dysfunctional but wasn't sure where to start the rehabilitation. Egos loomed large. Money loomed even larger—everyone wanted a share of the pie. There were so many overlapping incentives and disincentives to disentangle, and I couldn't trust the advice received from all sides in the "great blame game." Much of that advice involved contract terminations, which I knew instinctively weren't the best option.

Mike's advice was different—it was music to my ears. He didn't give me a consultant speech; he simply affirmed what I knew to be the problem but didn't know how best to tackle. In keeping with his straight-shooter style, Mike told me, "Nobody is working together, in fact everyone hates each other. I can help you build one team that shares success, problems, and solutions." I trusted him immediately, and at the end of our first meeting, I was ready to hire him. It took a bit of heavy lifting with our governance group who were skeptical about external "white knights," given our panoply of problematic contractors, but we got the ball rolling, and Mike arrived with a small team a few weeks later. He had an immediate impact, employing many of the techniques and methods outlined here in *It's All About Your Team*.

Trust is fragile in construction. Mike highlights various factors that break down trust, including standard processes such as RFIs and entitlement reviews. There is an irony that processes are often designed to foster accountability, and yet in doing so, they (inadvertently) undermine trust. This is especially apparent when the process starts to "wag the dog," so to speak.

A good example highlighted in *It's All About Your Team* is when the contract is used as a hammer, and the focus of the team inevitably turns away from project execution to enforcement of contractual provisions. Good governance and process are all well and good but not if they lead to a case of one step forward, two steps back. After all, it is people, not process, that get things done.

What is Mike's magical fairy dust? Construction is complicated, life is complicated, and the various chapters in *It's All About Your Team* bring out his approach and no-nonsense, practical problem-solving mentality:

You identify a problem, find options to solve it, make a selection, and act quickly and decisively to implement it.

That said, there is a secret ingredient—a powerful spice that boils down to fashioning a team from a bunch of egos with diverse incentives. It helps that Mike is a natural optimist, and his positive spin on difficult issues is infectious and helps build momentum for incremental progress. His reputation for "pizza diplomacy" on our project was a great signaling tool: the better the pizza at a meeting, the more difficult the issues to be resolved!

Building a team isn't easy. A construction team is not simply akin to a football team. It's like trying to fashion a unified team from four different sports to play a match on an unfamiliar pitch. Think of assembling a group of baseball, cricket, rugby, and football players and getting them to work together to play some sort of made-up combination game. Crafting such a team requires distilling many of the lessons from Mike's career: changing mindsets, a new culture, parking egos and pride, enhanced professionalism and collaboration, and a willingness to accept new accountability.

Moreover, it requires a shared and singular focus on getting out of your comfort zone and playing together because that is what matters. So it is for successful construction: everyone cares about the project above all else, and everyone has everyone else's back.

In conclusion, it is fitting that I highlight my singular admiration for Mike's ability to comprehend his client (a key piece of advice in *It's All About Your Team*). We were not an easy client, and I know he was often exasperated. But Mike the Disruptor remained true to his mantras and was always honest, open, consistent, and blunt with me. I so valued, trusted, and respected his advice and counsel. Thank you, my friend.

**–Chris Hemus**

*To my beloved wife, Lisa, and children, Daniela, Arianna, and Michelle; my partner, Farid Cardozo; and to all those who challenge the status quo; to my teammates; and to the beautiful journey that brought me here, thank you.*

# Preface

This book is a culmination of my life's work. The stories I tell highlight key moments of my construction, project, and program management career. The lessons I share, however, are about people. Whether it's business or family, our whole lives revolve around how we interact with, respond to, learn from, and grow alongside people. Each of the stories I've selected to share here emphasizes a different learning experience -- the culmination of which inspired this book -- and the takeaways are universal.

You can call them projects or deliverables or campaigns or sprints. Regardless of industry, we're talking about the same thing: *goals and objectives*–scope, schedule, budget, quality, and benefit requirements. The leadership and management strategies I outline can be similarly applied to produce the best value outcomes for each of these buckets.

I started in construction in Texas in 1978. At that time, the person on the job site who received the most attention was the biggest, burliest, most foul-mouthed person on the project. You know, the one who drops *f-bombs* twice in every breath. But the industry didn't earn its reputation because of one person; that was the culture.

Disagreements, conflict, and colorful language -- this was, and often still is, all standard fare. As I got older, I realized that I had to break what I saw as already broken to change how successful projects would proceed.

I was in ninth grade the first time anyone referred to me as "disruptive."

I was not what you'd call "a pleasure to have in class," so I didn't go and failed gym. As punishment, I was sent to that gym every day for the remainder of high school. Guess what? I have been working out for fifty-three years now.

That "failure" changed my life.

All of my failures changed my life in some way. I went through the various stages of pissing people off, then being a demanding and unreasonable boss, to being the champion of One Team. Shared Success.ˢᵐ This philosophy has changed my life and the way people work around me.

Last year, I was recognized as a Fifty Over 50 "Age Disruptor" in New York by City & State New York. I went from being disruptive to being a disruptor. You can imagine how good that felt.

All of these events left an impression on me. My work and the people around me over the past fifty years have taught me so much, and in this book, I share the experiences and stories about lifetime friends I have made by treating people with trust, respect, and dignity and giving 1,000 percent to every project. Unfortunately, I did not have the space to mention all the people who contributed to the success of these projects, because there are so many. It is worth noting, however, that these stories offer just a small window into a career that is richer as a result of all the people I have learned from along the way.

We shared the One Team. Shared Success.ˢᵐ experience.

# Contents

# CHAPTER 1

# Why Do Projects Succeed or Fail?

Throughout the course of my career, I've seen many things I like and many things I don't like. In fact, I've become a disrupter of the so-called "best practices" that have existed in the industry for decades. This disruptive attitude required that I detour around several obstacles and make changes that left some people uncomfortable at first. It also significantly affected numerous projects–they were done more quickly, efficiently, and profitably.

## The Cornerstones

I have come to a conclusion expressed in this book's title: It is *all* about your team.

In business, it's *all* about your team. This surprises some people. They think it's all about the dream or the vision or the impact, but it all boils down to who is going to get you there.

Your team begins with you.

Your team needs proactive human-centric leadership to support and encourage success.

Your team must focus on solving problems and removing obstacles.

As a leader, you become the project manager (PM), and the success of the project--including its goals and objectives--relies on you. What do you need to think about long before you schedule the first meeting, turn the first shovel, or prepare the first deliverable?

- The scope–in construction, the size and location, but more broadly the parameters
- The budget
- The schedule--not just when the final product is due, but each micro-deadline along the way
- The team that will execute

These are the four cornerstones of any project in any industry. The first is, of course, conceptualization or the vision of the result. The second is the planning stages, showing how you intend to reach the goals. The third is the design stage. The fourth is the execution stage, taking it from the theoretical to the actual.

To understand the vision, you have to look at the client internally–to get inside the client's head. You must understand their thinking about and goals for the project. You must comprehend the client to meet their needs and wants. This includes other stakeholders who will decide how a project ultimately takes shape.

Much of what they *need* will be decided by building codes. Other needs will be defined by the laws of physics–stable foundations, girder sizes, door sizes, wiring and piping, and so on. These are the things you largely can't change, try as you might -- and trust me, they will ask you to try.

Most of their *wants* are reasonable, especially if the client is an oil magnate with wealth gushing out of the ground. If not, budgets, timetables, and other considerations might prevent the dream from coming together exactly as envisioned. In such cases, the PM–a relentless realist–must let the client down gently but firmly, explaining that materials can be swapped and building inspectors can make exceptions, but Sir Isaac Newton can't be bribed.

Bent Flyvbjerg, the most cited scholar in the world on megaprojects, created a database of over 16,000 projects across various fields and industries spanning 136 countries. His research found that only 8.5 percent of projects meet both cost and time targets, and a mere 0.5 percent achieve cost, time, and benefit goals. Flyvbjerg put into data what I had never experienced first-hand. It was an eye-opener for me: 91.5 percent exceed budget, schedule, or both, while 99.5 percent surpass budget, schedule, benefits, or a combination thereof -- which underscores the rarity of projects adhering to their intended parameters.[1] Failure is standard fare.

Let's be clear: When you do not deliver a new hospital on time, you fail its patients. When you do not complete a new airport terminal as designed, you fail its travelers. And this is not just a construction industry problem. When a bank overspends on illiquid assets, it fails its customers. When our politicians cannot work together, they fail us as voters. Why do we continue to let this happen? My career -- and ultimately this book -- is motivated by the glaring need for a process to fix this culture of and apathy toward failure.

In construction, we must also look at projects externally. For example, if a town wanted a new hospital, why not take the mayor and other leaders to tour existing hospitals in similar communities and ask, "What do you like? What don't you like?" The PM should meet with some of the doctors, nurses, and other staff to learn what they want. In some cases, nurses understand better than doctors what it takes to do the job! In doing this research, you make certain that the client understands everything they're getting into, and you get alignment on all points. Everyone's on the same page.

While all this goes on, practical factors must be decided. For example, the PM has to ensure that proper governance is in place to execute the project: Can they pay the bills? Do they have sufficient resources ready and available? In your contracts, you need to get down to the real nitty-gritty details, like having accounting set up to get the checks written, signed, and delivered on time. Such things sound mundane (because they are) but never forget: In business, profit is gold, but cash flow is life or death.

If you start with solid cornerstones and pay attention to all the details, both cash flow and profit will follow.

---

[1]  Flyvbjerg, B., Gardner, D. (2023). *How Big Things Get Done*. Currency.

## The Team

### Good Soldiers

Bent Flyvbjerg's mega-project philosophy is centered around eleven heuristics, or rules, about the critical focus areas that determine the quality of the outcome or delivery. He starts with hiring a master builder, getting your team right, thinking slow and acting fast, watching the downside, saying no, making lifelong friends, doing climate mitigation, and admitting that your biggest risk is you. These heuristics spoke to me because they each touch on factors that you can control. Most notably, they all start and end with the team -- from leadership to specialized talent.

Flyvbjerg's principles, based on decades of research, affirmed my career-long observations:

1.  It's all about your team.
2.  If you ignore that, your project will fail and fail miserably.

This philosophy, whether you're building a highway or navigating a merger, will keep you and your team on target.[2] How am I so certain? There is an old proverb: "Gold won't always get you good soldiers, but good soldiers will always get you gold."[3] If it's true in war, it's certain enough for me.

With a preliminary scope, a preliminary budget, and a preliminary schedule—all defined by contract—you stand on square one. Now you must rally your troops, who will oversee your latest miracle and bring it home—on time, within budget, and in full compliance with the law and contract.

---

[2]  Flyvbjerg, B., Gardner, D. (2023). *How Big Things Get Done*. Currency.

[3]  The exact quote is, "I maintain, therefore, that it is not gold, as is vulgarly supposed, that is the sinews of war, but good soldiers; for while gold by itself will not gain you good soldiers, good soldiers may readily get you gold," from Niccolo Machiavelli, *Discourses on Livy*, 1531.

Distilling all these details into an effective plan can be a challenging exercise, because your original definition of the project's goals and objectives must now take into account dozens, if not hundreds or thousands, of people. It's no longer just about what the CEO wants; the execution and outcome relies on a plan that provides what everybody needs and as much of what everybody wants as possible. It must get all those with a stake in line.

Groan all you want, but team-building exercises are as important as properly lubricating an engine. As a leader, it's your responsibility to help them get to know one another and promote strong working partnerships by establishing trust, collaboration, accountability, open communications, and an understanding of how each individual will share in the success. This foundation is critical.

Your invitation to the key players' team depends on the role you play. A PM is usually tasked with determining what's needed and forming the team accordingly. The selected key players must be able to manage personnel and materials, with a constant eye toward scope, schedule, quality, and budget. The party responsible for execution should be involved in assembling the team in order to evaluate and confirm these capabilities on the front end. This is especially important for projects that require certain specialty players, which can be easily overlooked.

In New York City, you need a project expeditor. Securing the right permits in the Big Apple involves so much work that it requires the full time and attention of an experienced red-tape cutter to get them all in place when they're needed. Expeditors are often retired NYC Building Department employees, and they can mean the difference between starting the project on time or not starting at all. Someone not familiar with this process or its impact on execution might discount the expeditor's place on the key player's team.

Whatever the makeup of the final roster, the team must meet regularly—I suggest at the end of each week—to be sure that they remain on the same page. As each week closes, the PM should ask those key players:

- What did we do this week to control scope, schedule, and budget?
- What will we do next week to control scope, schedule, and budget?
- What risks were identified and what are the plans to mitigate them?

Then pay attention to the answers!

The CM, on the other hand, is usually among the last to be hired before labor is set to begin. By then, many of the biggest decisions have already been made, but the responsibility is largely the same: bring the team together and keep them together. The CM must integrate with the team that has been assembled and determine how to contribute. Meet the other key players, and begin building individual relationships.

These roles -- the PM and the CM -- exist in every business's hierarchy. The PM may be an executive vice president that reports to the CEO, or it could be a very hands-on CEO. The CM may be somewhere else in the line, working with what they have within the overall structure. Both of these roles have the power to enact change. What I've described above is the ideal scenario: the PM selects all the right key players and champions their progress. But what if the PM chose wrong? Or tells everyone, "Figure it out. Let me know when you're done"? The CM may not be in charge of the whole team, but they can influence how that team moves forward. A leader doesn't have to be the one on top.

## Team Culture

When structuring a team, how important is team culture for those involved? It is the essence of building a team. The team must foster trust, collaboration, and shared goals among its members.

Some managers want yes-men; good PMs never pretend they have all the answers, nor should they trust people who think they do. I prefer people who express their opinions, because you never know what they might have to teach you.

If a situation arises that a PM has never dealt with before, somebody else on the team probably has. When I ask questions, I expect intelligent answers—simple, direct answers based on experience or training. That's how you deal with problems efficiently. That question might go to a manager, supervisor, or those "down in the trenches." Sometimes calling in an outside consultant can give everyone a fresh set of eyes on a situation. The goal is to implement a solution, not for one individual to have the answer - or all the answers. That's what I mean by team culture.

The culture on most construction sites is one of conflict. There can be upward of forty different teams involved, yet they often do not function as one. Imagine a team sport where instead of collaborating, two teams compete against each other with supporters rooting for opposite sides. It's detrimental to progress and creates no room for resolution.

The Myers-Briggs Company's "CCP Global Human Capital Report: Workplace Conflict and How Businesses Can Harness It to Thrive," found out that 85 percent of employees continue to encounter conflict at work, and the average time spent addressing it has escalated significantly. Employees now spend approximately 4.34 hours each week on conflict (2022), a sharp rise from the 2.8 hours recorded in 2008. In 2008, this equated to approximately $359 billion in paid hours (Bureau of Labor Statistics, May 2008), and considering the rate escalation, this figure could exceed $1 trillion in today's dollars. The frequency of conflict has also risen, with 36 percent of workers regularly facing conflict, up from 29 percent in 2008.[4]

Despite this growing challenge, the report emphasizes that the focus for management should not be on avoiding conflict but rather on managing it effectively. The report cautions that ignoring the need for effective conflict management strategies can lead

---

[4] CPP Inc. and OPP Ltd. (2008). "CCP Global Human Capital Report: Workplace Conflict and How Businesses Can Harness It to Thrive." CPP, Inc.; https://img.en25.com/Web/CPP/Conflict_report.pdf

to significant negative impacts—financially, operationally, and on employee well-being.[5]

This is why project teams should prioritize conflict resolution and create support systems to safeguard against project instability. Always try to deal with problems at the most practical level—that is, where changes can be implemented most quickly and effectively. The last thing you want to do is get lost in the weeds and waste time. Part of the team culture, therefore, must be trust—you must trust them enough to seek their advice, and they must trust you enough to give it.

The same is true for problem solving. A good PM wants people who'll speak up when they have problems, even personal ones. No one can find a solution if they don't know what's wrong. Distractions happen—children, parents, illnesses—and an important part of the culture should be caring about and helping co-workers so they can stay focused and on schedule.

Consider a scenario where a team member is struggling with work-load while dealing with a sick parent. In the right environment, they feel comfortable discussing these challenges with the PM, who acknowledges the difficulty of the situation. Together, they prioritize urgent project tasks and adjust where feasible. This openness not only helps them manage both personal and professional responsibilities more effectively, but also reinforces a culture of trust and support within the team.

The more people a PM is responsible for, the more important that trust becomes. You have to know that someone will take responsibility, do what they need to do, and report back without being micro-managed. As long as the overarching goals are met, why shouldn't they be free to run their day in a way that works best for them? We rely on the architect to do that job and design properly and the

---

[5] The Myers-Briggs Company. (2022). Conflict at work: a research report. The Myers-Briggs Company, https://www.themyersbriggs.com/en-US/Programs/Conflict-at-Work-Research

engineers to certify their drawings—everything they're expected to do is part of the criteria for hiring them. Professionals must be professional every step of the way.

In construction, we tend to encounter the perception that there's a difference between the trades and the professions. There are some differences in the jobs themselves, but the expectation of professionalism—knowing your role and always doing your best—must apply equally to every team member. As project managers or champions, we lead by creating the team and the culture that allows every person to do exactly that and be rewarded properly. That driving mentality keeps every worker happy and excited about being on the job and doing their best every day.

Professionalism on all levels creates the ultimate win-win scenario.

## The Inevitable

Unlike fairy tales and Hollywood musicals, it's never "and they lived happily ever after."

Every project runs into problems, and people are often the root of those problems. On any team, there's a mix of personalities and attitudes. You don't have to become the best of friends, but you do have to work together courteously and professionally.

I find that when you sit people down and lay out your expectations, they will usually correct their attitude or actions in time. Sometimes people need to be made aware of what behaviors are contributing to challenges for the rest of the team - I've encountered many individuals in my career who simply didn't know that what they were doing was wrong or causing problems down the line for other people.

I've also learned that not everyone comes around. Not everyone wants to be part of a team, and in those cases, I have no choice but to replace them.

When people come up short, you part ways, remembering the words of Don Corleone, "It's not personal, it's just business."[6] Our team is creating a product for a client. If a team member doesn't contribute sufficiently to that goal, the rest of us can't be sentimental.

There are many reasons to watch the cornerstones carefully, and people taking advantage of you can be high on that list. I've had to replace subcontractors when I was CM, and I've let tradesmen go, because they were not cooperating, or they were abusing the budget. In signing a contract as PM or CM, you assume steward-ship—the responsibility to oversee and protect the interests of the client. You're legally and ethically bound to make sure the client's getting fair value and not being taken for a ride.

The entire workforce is a team made up of many smaller teams. You want everybody to enjoy coming to work each day and to earn a fair wage for fair effort because that's what you want for yourself. When one person (or a few people) has a problem, the CM or PM must fix that problem. That includes removing people if they become obstacles to success. Every boardroom, every jobsite, every place

---

[6] *The Godfather*, written by Mario Puzo and Francis Ford Coppola, directed by Francis Ford Coppola, Columbia Pictures, 1972.

of business must have clear standards that every member of every team understands and agrees to abide by.

The decision to ask someone to leave should never be yours. It should have been theirs.

## Quality

Quality is also within our control and must be managed from the initial planning until the final handover. PMs maintain quality by keeping one eye on what should be and the other on what is. How does the PM know that the project is running the way it should? When I walk onto a project site in the morning, I can usually feel it, because I look for details:

- When you see a dirty site—junk and debris lying all over the place—lack of organization is your first clue.
- When you see tools and equipment not being properly cared for, you know they'll need more frequent service or replacement.
- When you see tools and equipment not properly stored, you know you have safety concerns.
- When supplies and materials are organized, you know you have enough and that it isn't being wasted.
- When people are working hard instead of sitting in a corner trying to figure out what to do next, you know the plan of the day is being followed.
- When you go to the office and see that reports are timely and they describe what's happening, not sugarcoating problems, you know supervisors and managers are doing their jobs correctly.
- When you meet with key players and you see them speaking respectfully to each other—even when discussing hard questions—you know they're focused on resolving issues instead of trying to prove "I was right" or saying, "I told you so."

There's a lot of talk these days about key performance indicators (KPIs)—stock prices, conversions, the number of bricks laid or whatever. There are also people-based KPIs, the ones that tell you if the team members respect themselves, their jobs, their teammates, and their client's money. When the team is meeting people-based KPIs, you'll see work that's highly efficient, high quality, and highly profitable.

*Quality Assurance and Quality Control*
Delivering high quality, I repeat, depends on actions that begin on Day One. People who come in at the end and say, "You did it wrong," are not as useful as those who catch mistakes before they are repeated or become costly to reverse. Frequently, construction companies (as well as others, I'm sure) have teams for both: quality control (QC) and quality assurance (QA). QC is on the front end; usually, the construction manager and his team. QA is on the back end, the inspectors.

I don't necessarily agree that is the most effective setup. To me, the logic is simple: With the QA people on the QC team, they see what's happening in real time. Instead of coming at the end and saying, "You need to do all of this over again," they can catch errors or inefficiencies in progress and say, "You need to do this differently moving forward."

The number one cause of failure is a delay.

Organize one blended QA/QC team with responsibility for preventing these delays. Who has to review and present the finished product? Who can serve as their eyes on the progress made while it's happening?

In construction, this team should be staffed with architects, engineers, and experienced construction personnel to review every aspect of the work from Day One. The goal is zero punch list items at the end -- no edits to the deck, no miscalculations in the spreadsheet, no last-minute after-hours cleanup. You may not, of course, meet that goal, but in striving for that level of perfection, you may get so close that you surprise even yourselves.

Starting with a good QA/QC unit keeps your whole team focused on resolving issues as they arise, reducing the amount of rework that's needed. You don't want to have to deal with a long list of little problems right at the end of the calendar. Fixing mistakes is costly and time-consuming and can get very costly if you're tight on time or money.

When I talk about team culture, this is what I am talking about. You want everyone to have everyone else's back, regardless of which vendor or department they came from, and that means everyone takes responsibility for quality. Anyone can see a mistake, and the people doing the work are most likely to see small, easy-to-fix mistakes and correct them before they become big, expensive ones. This also means hiring people who pay attention and providing ongoing training. No matter how long you've been doing something, you need to keep your tools sharp.

Creating the expectation of and accountability for quality can be a challenge, but it becomes habitual. Start by teaching your team that when you leave a room, the work is done—not 95 percent done; done! Advocate for the mindset that everything is a micro project that's part of a mini project that's part of a major project, and all of which are part of the big project. Motivate them to complete that micro project like they're going to sign their name on it for all the world to see. That's behavior that breeds quality, and you can train that behavior in people. If someone is executing their piece and managing the work like they own the company, that's quality. On the flip side, when you go into a room or meeting and the noise is disruptive, but none of it's focused on topics that need discussion, how is the project going to get delivered?

### Basic Elements of QA/QC

The most essential element of QA/QC is ensuring it is managed by people that know what to look for. They should be evaluating progress as they would if the project were complete: "Is this correct? Does this belong here? Has this satisfied the ask?" I've always been amused that people say both, "God is in the details," and, "The devil's in the details." Both are true; it's the little things that can make or break a project.

QA/QC people must know what's wrong; they have to know how things should be done and recognize when they aren't done correctly. This is a quality that I always look for in supervisors and managers. It's one thing to get a job done on time and under budget and meet the quality expectations; it's quite another to get it done on time when the budget and quality goals are not met.

As leaders, we have to be able to rely on that next layer of management as a filter. The CEO can't be on the QA/QC team; a lot of us would be out of a job if they were, but the whole team structure is in place so that they don't have to be. Effective supervisors and managers not only spot and correct problems themselves, but also provide feedback straight-up to their reports so they can learn, as well.

"Why is this piece missing?"

"Oh, we don't want to do it until the end, because of this and that."

"But if you wait until the end, it's going to take two weeks longer to get done, and you won't get any added quality. You can do that work up front and protect it while you work around it."

How does the supervisor or manager know that? Training and experience!

> *Quality is not an act; it is a habit.*
> *—Will Durant[7]*

In construction, QA/QC folks don't simply know how to build—they also *really* know how to design and build *properly*. In fact, many

---

[7] Often attributed to Aristotle, it certainly reflects his attitude, but this verbiage was first published in Will Durant, *The Story of Philosophy: The Lives and Opinions of the World's Greatest Philosophers*. New York City: Simon & Schuster, 1926.

project managers in this industry have past lives in other related professions, and it makes their eye for detail that much stronger. Then there are people whose trade is their craft; they can look at the design and see it in their minds so clearly that when they get to the jobsite, they recreate it just as they envisioned it. All of these roles are equally important for delivery and must be respected as such.

When they're keyed toward professionalism, architects, engineers, general contractors, carpenters, electricians, and other trades work together smoothly. Moreover, you'll hear a lot of people saying things like, "That outlet cover was installed crooked" or "That wire we pulled is too short." You won't see people getting upset about it. It's not a criticism—it is a critique and an honest effort to help others do their best. We catch mistakes and correct them as we go, avoiding our worst nightmare—having to rip up good work to redo bad work.

I mentioned previously that, at times, having "outsiders" come in and do a quick check now and then can be a helpful exercise. Getting a fresh pair of eyes on the problem is an idea so old as to be a cliché, but we keep repeating clichés because they keep turning out to be true. Architects, designers, and engineers spend most of their time in offices - as do most finance, marketing, and IT professionals. Putting them in the field regularly does two things: first, they experience what the vision/goal is supposed to be so they can explain it most clearly; second, they are reminded of the actual, as well as the theoretical, limitations of exactly what the trades can do.

Drawings are flat pieces of paper or data points on a display. They represent ideas in one mind that we want to communicate to other minds. There's never perfect communication, because we're human. The architects and engineers know what they want to see as "quality." Designers know the intent and should regularly brief the teams with, "This is what I envisioned. This is what we're trying to accomplish here. We've outlined this in these drawings; let me answer any questions you might have."

Reinforcing the message is key to internalizing the message.

*Sampling and Mockery*

Professional consultants with specialized expertise can also bring immense value to the QA/QC team. If you're working in an earth-quake-prone locale for the first time, it might be prudent to hire a seismic regulations expert. Hazardous materials data sheets change frequently with ongoing research, so hire a specialist with knowl-edge of those changes.

Sometimes, the best insight comes from those who will deal with the outcome of a project most directly -- the end user. Will it work? They'll know if it doesn't, so their feedback is priceless in getting it right.

If you're building a hospital, for example, should you ask the recep-tionist how to design the reception area? Absolutely! That person has to work there, interact with staff and patients, give directions, keep an eye on the waiting room—just in case a non-critical patient suddenly goes critical—and so on. Is the space big enough for all the paperwork or computers? Can it accommodate the anticipated daily patient inflow? Is the room welcoming and calming? Does it provide for parents who must bring several children with them?

Should you ask doctors and nurses what they need in an operating room? Absolutely! They need major technologies in place, such as instruments, tools, and emergency equipment—in addition to space for additional nurses or surgeons. If it's a teaching hospital, there may be a second-floor gallery for students in some operating rooms. Do the personnel have enough space for all their gear and for them to move around comfortably? Do the students have good sight lines for observations? Will a video system be installed for close-ups of the latest techniques in microsurgery?

You may be lucky and have several existing spaces to sample. They may say, "We like this space. This operating room [this exam room, this procedure room, etc.] meets our needs perfectly." Great, clone it!

If not, it can be very cost-effective to mock it up, because most people can't visualize drawings. When they see a mock-up, they can experience being in a real space. Build it full-scale off-site with cardboard boxes, folding tables, and other inexpensive stand-ins, then walk people through it. Build the mock-up so that walls and equipment can move easily within it, then adjust things until the end users are satisfied that it will work. (If, after that, it doesn't, it's on them, not on you!) If you've made it as realistic as possible for them, the real one will work just as well.

If you built it and somebody then walks in and says it's not big enough, there's not much you can do about that. You may have built it exactly to the specifications they requested, but if in the final analysis it doesn't work, everybody starts over—with negotiation over "fault" (something one never admits to), cost estimates for replacement work and who'll bear them, and the incidental costs of those delays. You'll save time, effort, and money by recreating the experience in a mock-up on the front end, while boosting satisfaction by knowing you're giving the client a product you've proven will work for them.

This process isn't only effective for a client or end user who isn't totally sure what they want or how it should look. Some people are very specific about what they want. The hardest ones that I encounter—and I run into them regularly—are doctors and bureaucrats, and they benefit just as much (if not more) from this visualization exercise.

Most hospitals have an imaging equipment manager who oversees the inventory of X-ray, MRI, CAT scan, and other vital machines. One of the doctors may be used to operating equipment from Siemens, instead of GE, and may prefer German engineering. A government owned or operated facility, however, may require the use of GE products to ensure taxpayers' dollars are spent on a US-based company.

The specifications—size, power requirements, etc.—of each machine are different and proprietary to their manufacturer. Even the base plates they sit on are unique to the manufacturer, so knowing which products need to go where is critical. You don't want to stop mid-installation to rework the electrical system or floor plan.

This is what *alignment* is all about. You are building a facility that houses employees, customers, machines, and more. The space must fit all of these needs, and it's easy to overlook the many nuances involved. If the machinery, as designed, doesn't fit or the people are uncomfortable, it's a hassle to go back and rebuild that room. That's not a change, but an unacceptable, unnecessary change—a delay that could damage profitability.

You prevent these kinds of scenarios with the QA/QC team: Tell the client up front the potential costs of changing things at the last minute. Make sure everybody's on the same page on all details. Walk around every week, with team members, specialists, the client, or end users, as appropriate, checking and signing off on everything you do. And when there are concerns, listen to them.

## We Have Learned by Sad Experience

The costliest change order I have ever experienced in my professional career was a perfect storm of all the potentials I've warned about here; the team didn't even come close to getting it right.

The promise of an airport's new baggage-handling system had made the place infamous. It was designed to be a state-of-the-art, electronically-based, no-human-error system completely controlled by GIS tracking. The problem? There were many:

- The system was based on unproven technology that had never been used on such a large scale.
- The system was designed with a network of conveyor belts, tracks, and automated carts to handle sixty-thousand bags per day, but far more luggage came through.
- The proper rights-of-way for the miles of baggage conveyors, belts, tracks, and accessories required were not included in the original design of the space in the terminal and concourses.
- The system was also not integrated with the check-in and flight-scheduling systems, so if a flight was delayed or rescheduled, it would fail to update the baggage routing data.

None of this was a secret. The client had been warned:

- At the onset of construction, a consultant told them the system was overly complex. They moved forward anyway.
- They established a timeline of just two years for full implementation. A smaller project at another airport had taken two years just to complete before another six months was spent in rigorous 24/7 testing before launch. Despite concerns about the feasibility of the timeline, they pressed ahead with that schedule.
- When the airport invited bids for building the system, none of the proposals could meet the deadline. The bids were rejected, and a completely different company was awarded the project without extending the timeline.
- Only 10 percent of the system's computer operating code had been written by the time the contract period was over halfway through--time that should have included testing and commissioning the code that was nowhere near complete. No changes were made to the programming staff or the schedule.

The system was ambitious, but it was far too complex -- and even if it could have been implemented with more time, it still wouldn't have been able to handle the airport's regular baggage volume, defeating its own purpose after all that trouble.

A change order of this size isn't any one person's fault; this colossal failure was the result of an accumulation of errors and omissions, design flaws, untested technology, and the lack of qualified professionals who could see these issues before they ballooned.

This was a big deal when it happened, and it earned worldwide attention -- unfortunately, all negative. After some time, the total cost of the baggage system had grown into more than double the original budget. Eventually, it was modified into a more traditional tug-and-cart model. The airport opened after more than one year of delays and $2 billion more than originally budgeted. It's now politely called a series of unnecessary mistakes. Time delays and the resulting exposure really are the costliest problems on any project.

This is true even on a smaller scale. We were once wrapping up the renovation of a large office building, and the architect was upset that the finishes on the walls didn't reach a "level 5." Level 5 is the highest standard of finish on a wall - *no* bumps, just a beautifully *smooth* wall. The trades insisted it was done to level 5; the architect was sure it wasn't. This is where a fresh set of eyes comes in handy. The Gypsum Association, the experts on drywall, came through, inspected, and documented the walls as level 5 finishes.

The contractor was the loudest voice in that debate because, though willing to do the work, he was not willing to redo work after doing it right the first time. After the association came in, everybody was aligned on the fact that it had been done properly. Fortunately, this was a simple fix–through additional training, the architect came to understand the standard and could make a proper appraisal of the product. That experience also helped to retrain the architect to look at walls differently moving forward, which eliminated further challenges to the quality of work.

Of course, some people will always say something negative, and somebody else will say, "Just take it off the list." They let things go, rather than arguing about or fixing them. These are people who've made themselves obstacles to success. When you have such an obstacle on a job, you need to remove it. Obstacles cause delays, and delays cost money, so don't hesitate to just say goodbye.

## Playing the Cards You're Dealt With

If the QA/QC team is handling its responsibilities properly, you will, almost certainly, see problems arise every single day. Effective QA/QC leadership means assessing the situation and assigning responsibility to mitigate it. Some problems are going to be so simple to solve that they hardly deserve to be called problems: somebody has a question about a drawing, or some piece of equipment is here but needs to be moved there. Others will be more serious: a large delivery is behind schedule, or a major machine breaks down.

Whatever the type or level of difficulty, these issues should be reported as soon as they are identified, so you have time that day to act on them. Failure to bring problems forward in a timely manner means failure to solve them in a timely manner.

In construction, we deal with two types of problems: human error and what are called "acts of God"—with appropriate apologies to nonbelievers. Acts of God are things like the weather—things we can't control. When the storm hits, work stops (as a safety precaution), and we pick it up again when the sun comes out. Human error is inevitable, but much of it is preventable. If you build the team so that everybody has each other's back—that is, they're truly working as a team—you'll prevent many failures because everybody is always inspecting their own and their co-workers' work, seeing problems, fixing them quickly, and explaining what went wrong so that it doesn't happen again.

## The Elevator Pitch

Regardless of the project or strategy or campaign you are delivering, the management process is the same; and if that's true, what meaningfully differentiates one project manager from another? What are you going to do differently? What special skills do you bring to the table?

My pitch to you is that it must be the team.

"If you hire me, you will see a difference, a workplace atmosphere that you've never seen before. You've never seen the cooperation of people the way it should be, because nobody does it. They all fight—everyone wants to fight. You hear people talk about integrated project delivery. It works well enough, but it's a contract-based system. I don't want to do it that way. I don't want a contract. I want people to live this collaborative ideal or, at least, strive for it. I want people to do it because they want to do it because they see the benefit of it."

When you start—from the first day on any job—by striving to make it a collaborative effort, with every person all in and working together, that's where you begin to differentiate yourself from the herd. In most projects, everybody focuses on their job and that job alone. That's why they're on the site. Getting them to think about other people's jobs and how they can help move those jobs forward can be uncomfortable at first, but it can also be contagious.

One team—shared success, shared problems, shared solutions.

That's the end of our day. My life's goal has been to build a culture of people who understand that, whenever you see something wrong, help fix it, and help others make it work.

It's not easy to change people's attitudes, and you'll find that I have not always been successful. Construction is a hard business, traditionally full of hard people and hard traditions. Even so, once the first person buys into the idea and starts showing real success with the system, others buy into it and share that success.

# CHAPTER 2

# Southwest Freeway in Houston, Texas (1987-1991)

*I want to dedicate this chapter to Lonnie Beckham, the lead TxDOT resident engineer; Donald Stankovsky, my mentor; and the rest of the team (contractors, engineers, TxDOT, METRO, etc.) I was so fortunate to work with. We all became close because every idea was considered, no matter where it originated, and we supported each other to make the system work better. They understood what I wanted to do and why I wanted to do it in a new way and they all contributed to the ultimate success. They had confidence and trust in our relationship and, more than anyone, they all made this a great project to be part of.*

Construction is historically a very competitive industry, and often still is. It's usually run as one team against another, which makes collaboration a very rare occurrence. Many large-scale infrastructure construction projects fall under the civil engineering category, which is sponsored and managed by municipal, county, state, or federal agencies—including highways, roads, bridges, tunnels, transit, and airports. Compounded by the combative nature of the business, these bureaucratically-run projects can create the potential for a headache the size of Mount Everest. As I learned throughout the course of my career, many of the problems that often arise can be avoided with the right organization.

One of my most successful—that is, most disruptive—projects is the expanded part of Interstate 59 (I-59)—called the Southwest Freeway in Houston, Texas, stretching from Shepherd Drive to the Sam Houston Tollway—a Texas State Highway commonly known as "Beltway 8."

When it began in 1987, I was a senior project manager for Houston's Mass Transit Agency, the Metro. The Texas Department of Transportation (TxDOT) wanted to expand the freeway from three lanes in each direction to seven and add a bus line in the middle of it all. The project was divided into four three-mile segments: three designed by Metro's design consultants and the fourth by TxDOT.

The plan, as originally laid out, contained three major traffic control phases. Phase I built the outside lanes, placing the frontage roads close to the right-of-way (ROW). Phase II constructed the new freeway lanes between the frontage road and the existing highway lanes. Phase III rebuilt the existing center lanes, including the addition of the bus lane.

TxDOT said the project would require six to seven years—I thought it could be done in three. TxDOT didn't believe me—that's one of the challenges when dealing with bureaucrats. Agency executives generally have experience in the field, but have been out of the hands-on work for a while and aren't up on the latest best practices. They're often used to dealing with red tape and delayed timelines while tending to lean toward the hardheaded. They also didn't have much of a reason to trust me.

"No, it's a six- to seven-year job," TxDOT insisted, but gave me a chance to prove it could be done. They hired a consultant from the University of Texas in Austin (UT Austin) to look over my shoulder while I did it. The consultant was also a former TxDOT District Engineer for Houston, the district we were building in—which meant I was being watched by someone with the same mentality and suspicions I was already up against.

## Research

I spent a year planning how it could be done, documenting every fact in my proposal. I met with people at every level of TxDOT, the UT Austin consultant, the Association of General Contractors (AGC) of Texas, and several others.

24

Delays are the number one cause of a project's failure, so my research included discovering how to avoid them. I started with the team itself, reviewing the work of all the engineers on the project. I went to the state records office and studied where change orders were executed against those engineers -- in other words, when their work required revision for some reason or another. There was one firm in particular that came to light - the same firm working on the section of the highway that I designed. They had an engineer on staff who made the same mistake more than ten times—one that resulted in change orders for every project he worked on. Sure enough, that engineer made the same mistake on our project as well, so we pulled the drawings and got them corrected. Then I went to that engineer and explained the situation.

"You made this mistake on the last ten projects you designed."

"What do you mean?"

I demonstrated.

There was genuine surprise. "Nobody's ever shown me that."

"Well, I'm showing you now, because I want you to be aware of what you did."

When people are ingrained in their day-to-day tasks, and aren't considering jobs beyond their own, it can be easy to overlook these kinds of patterns. The key to getting the best out of your team is to ensure that these patterns aren't repeated, benefiting you and everyone they work with down the road. This is the first step in getting people to work better together.

I also looked at where the change orders came from in another project that TxDOT built concerning traffic control. I saw errors, omissions from engineers, and mistakes in drawings where critical information was left out. All of these things would have caused delays down the line had they not been addressed when I discovered them. I had TxDOT update all the drawings and correct all those omissions before we even got started. From there we had a great design to move us forward, and we knew it because we'd done the research. That vastly changed the flavor of the project—we never ran into the issue of workers saying, "We can't do this, because the designs are wrong," in the middle of construction, because we'd gotten ahead of it.

These activities were not a traditional procedure for TxDOT, the engineers, or for us. I created disruption in the process.

I told TxDOT, "You do a great job managing construction. You know exactly what has to be done. You pay attention to quality control, but you don't focus on the sequence of what has to be built. That's a problem. Focus on what has to be built," in an effort to change their mindset. One day, I got there and showed them some tasks. "That's getting done next week."

They said, "How do you know that?"

"My schedule shows everything."

This, too, was a new concept for them. TxDOT had often said, and said on this project, "No, schedules don't help us." In fact, contractors had frequently used schedules against the State Department of Highways and Public Transportation for overpayments. Once an owner or agency approves a contractor's schedule, regardless of its accuracy, the contractor can use any deviation from the timeline as a means of negotiating higher fees to account for the delay -- even if their errors or mistakes in the original schedule are to blame. This happens all the time in construction, and it's something I was not going to allow to happen here.

I told TxDOT that schedules have a huge value when used correctly. "We're going to use schedules to manage the project. We're not using it to beat people up. We're going to own this schedule and make it work for us." Then I demonstrated what I meant.

The problem was data. Not a lack of data—they had piles of it, but nobody ever looked at it. I found the data I needed and used it to build a schedule that could execute the job the way I'd proposed. The UT Austin consultant and the AGC backed me up. When they agreed it could be done, TxDOT got on board.

After that year's worth of planning, we started developing the team. I had initially only been brought on as a project manager for one of the segments but felt we could be most effective as the executive construction manager, which would involve overseeing the entire build. This was new to TxDOT and it probably made them nervous to entrust that much responsibility to one entity. That proposal was how I started to change the culture of the typical TxDOT project. They had resident engineers and inspectors whose role was to inspect the quality of the project, making sure the contractors were follow-ing the drawings and specifications. My focus was not on inspection, but on how to build it better, faster, and to achieve the results they wanted in addition to those I wanted. We were showing them how to build the project—how many people were needed, where all the lane closures and timing would be, and where inspections had to be done.

When you build any kind of horizontal project, detailed traffic control drawings are required to identify the closure of the work area. That requires you to take a segment of highway out of commission and use half the remaining lanes for each direction of travel. After you've rebuilt the closed section, you reopen it and move on to the next segment. That was also a role I felt I could provide the most value in, and TxDOT agreed.

I presented my schedule to their resident engineers and showed them a software package I'd developed to help oversee the project; I took an off-the-shelf product scheduling system (called Open Plan back then) and had the company revise it to base the schedule durations on quantities of material, production rates for each material, and crew sizes. For example, if you're pouring concrete at thirteen inches thick, you need a crew of X number of people to work Y number of hours to prepare and pour every yard of concrete. We built those production rates into our schedule. So, when somebody went through and said, "I need to pour concrete from this place to that place," we could tell him exactly how many crew members he'd need and how long it should take.

By doing this, we had solid research that gave us realistically achievable, real-world KPIs we could easily measure when we got into the field and on the job. With the concrete pour, for example, I knew that they needed seven people, so we set the expectation that seven people should be on the job. If we inspected the worksite and saw only three, the math wouldn't add up. They weren't going to make their production for that day. We, then, could say, "Listen, you don't have enough people here to meet your schedule." We took pictures every day, at every activity, and recorded why those pictures were taken.

## Build a Reasonable Schedule

I don't need to tell anybody reading this that construction workers can be a rough bunch. Tough men and women doing hard work are generally not the type to care about the opinions of others. Using our system, a lot of the usual BS involving cut corners and silly mistakes went away, because they knew (and I heard), "No, these guys are watching every minute and protecting the best interest of the project."

We wanted to get things done. We didn't care about what it took to get what we wanted, because what we wanted was reasonable by design. The record for the Transcontinental Railroad was ten miles of track laid in one day. How they did that when the average was one foot per day,[8] I have no idea, and I don't care. I didn't set my schedule based on "ten-mile days"; I built it based on "one-foot days." That way, nobody had any excuses for not doing their part.

We never kept this a secret. It was the expectation, and everyone was aligned on what it was. "There's the schedule," we told them, "And it's meant to be kept. It's based entirely on achievable production—enough to meet the established average to keep the rest of us on schedule. If you can't, tell us how we can help you get there."

The schedule was built around traffic control plans, defining the areas of work for each segment. When I first took over the entire project for Metro, I formed a traffic control working group with all the design consultants. I put the most qualified person in charge and told them what the mission was. The plan was to standardize the process and organize the work around the most efficient staging and sequencing—bigger work areas that were aligned between all the four segments. The interface points are where the most risk is, and we had a way to deal with them. This was the most significant change to allow schedule efficiency and alignment.

It worked!

## Team Culture

Having seen the schedule and the logic that went into its development, TxDOT, the contractors, and the rest of the project team agreed the three-year timeline I had initially proposed was, in fact,

---

[8] "Building the Transcontinental Railroad," *DigitalHistory.UH.edu*. Houston TX: University of Houston, 2021. https://www.digitalhistory.uh.edu/disp_textbook.cfm?smtID=2&psid=3147#:~:text=The%20progress%20in%20the%20tunnels,10%20miles%20in%20a%20day, accessed 12 December 2023.

possible. The job took off, and it was very well-executed because our team culture was amazing. Once they understood the sequencing, they started to see that if we built it this way, we'd get a better result in the end. That became our mindset: we planned the job, we executed the plan, everyone involved used the system and data developed, and we crushed it.

We made every milestone and every date for the next three years. It was a very successful project--almost no change orders, on-time quality delivery, and the traffic was controlled. The federal government had funded a large portion of the project, so they kept their eyes on us to ensure we wouldn't incur costly delays. I believe they estimated the delay would cost $250,000 per day, so we worked very hard to make sure nobody incurred those costs.

Some of that hard work was with the higher-ups of TxDOT. They hadn't met me when I started, didn't know what I'd done, and they were very hesitant to let me and my wild ideas loose on their project. They resisted my ideas for a long time, but by the end, they came to understand what I tried to do. In other projects, the schedule had been a problem for them. It had been a tool that contractors used against TxDOT in order to file claims. I turned that around when I suggested, "No, this is a tool to build the project. Let's manage the schedule, manage the delays right out of existence, and get everybody to work as a team." That's what happened, and the job got done. In the end, it was a pretty impressive sight–the new Southwest Freeway opened on time, with just a half percent of the budget spent on change orders in one of the segments.

## Converts

Once the culture was established and the two TxDOT resident engineers saw what we were doing, they liked the success we achieved and joined in. From there, my life as a PM became extremely easy. They would listen, they would act, and they would work with the contractor to mitigate the delays and issues we were having. That became an everyday thing, and it never became about whose fault it was.

In fact, it became an interesting challenge for them. I remember conversations where each of the schedules for every part of the job were discussed. That's what they were afraid of—claims and delays—because those would cost them money, but we ended up with essentially none. It was all about attitude:

"How do we get this contractor to work if we're in the way? Let's get out of the way. Let's help them put this thing to bed," was the mentality. We set physical timelines that were all met, even when we knew they were going to be a challenge. We had the data that showed it could be done. At one point, for example, we decided to align traffic control in all four sections. We wanted to do one, big traffic control switch—from the existing highway to the temporary construction route—in one day. I admit even I thought it was impossible. However, when we aligned all the contractors, they actually got it done.

When the project rounded out in 1991, several said to me, "Mike, we made more money because you motivated people to get it done. They worked harder, and none of them wanted to be that guy that was late. They performed."

Construction projects are often a struggle because so many things can go wrong. This project was not a struggle with the culture we'd built and the right mindsets in place; it was a huge win-win all around.

## My Role

What was I doing throughout all this? What was my biggest workload for this project?

As PM, I had to coordinate all those drawings throughout the whole project. I had to get everything to link up while creating and maintaining that harmonious culture. The traffic control switches I mentioned could've been a major headache and a significant cost—about $200,000 every time we had to redirect traffic from one part of the highway to another through those infamous S-curves. We found a way to align all those segments. The savings from not having to switch back and forth between sections totaled almost $1 million (and a lot of valuable time). Most of that money ended up in the pockets of contractors as added incentives for continued quality—another win-win scenario. This was referred to as the "Big Switch."

All of it stemmed from the team culture and mindset. Working together and helping each other to achieve more, instead of competing against each other, allowed every team to share success. When all was said and done, everybody knew they'd achieved a great feat.

## My Partner

The word "culture," in this context, isn't that old. When I started out in this industry, that word and attitude wasn't on anybody's mind. I think "culture" only rose to commonplace in the last ten years or so. I love the word--it's a great way to describe how teams work (or don't). I remember one of the resident engineers on the project, Lonnie Beckham; he was about sixty-five years old and an expert in the field. When our formal relationship was new, he'd say, "Let me see your schedule." So, I'd show him my schedule, and he'd reply, "Mike, what I'm seeing is exactly what I feel, but I can't express it the way you're doing it." We became great friends. He was my advocate and partner. We actually shared the same birthday. In fact, the first day we met, he said, "Let me show you something."

He took me to the field. Now, you have to understand that this guy was a very experienced resident engineer. He knew how to build-- he didn't think about what order to build in, but he knew how to build. When we got to a certain place, he said, "You see that right here? You see where this water is at this intersection?" I did. "That's where the contractor is going to start."

"What do you mean, Lonnie?"

"Well, they always start where they can't start."

*That's a problem*, I thought to myself, so I said, "Why don't we make them start where we want them to start? We show them the schedule. We work with the schedule. We work with them to meet the schedule. We can tell them anything we want in the beginning. Once it's locked down, then we're pretty much stuck with it. We could still change a few things, but let's try and start everything off right the first time."

"So, we can go there and tell them to start on the south side instead of the north side?"

"Absolutely."

As I said, bureaucrats can be hardheaded, always doing things the way they were done in the past and expecting the same outcomes as before. With this new process in place, Lonnie changed his attitude about how contractors work, a part of a new culture of cooperation. It's funny; I had no idea what "culture" meant back then, but we changed everybody's attitudes, which shifted the atmosphere on the project. The contractors were very skeptical in the beginning, so we didn't force anything down their throats. We just showed them what it would do, worked with them, and moved obstacles for them. When they started to see that they could make more money doing it as we suggested, they were suddenly, but not at all surprisingly, on board with the new culture.

However, the most exciting thing about the whole process was something you might never guess—nobody cared about making more money. They focused on what they needed to do to get the project completed on time, the first time. The Southwest Freeway project was the biggest operation any of us had ever been part of. Even after we passed a point where we knew it was going to get finished successfully, their enthusiasm never slowed down. That might be the most fantastic part of the whole activity. And the money? There were plenty of bonuses paid out. The team found that if they focused on getting the job done right, the money naturally flowed in afterward.

## The Big Difference

As you'll continue to see, I'm a really big fan of scheduling if you use it as a tool, not as a weapon. In the past, TxDOT had problems because they didn't understand scheduling as a tool. The contractors only created a schedule because it's a piece of paper they're

33

required to have, and they only used it when it could benefit them financially. The resident engineers mostly just put it in a drawer. They rarely looked at it, they never understood it, and never made it an advantage.

I put it up on the screen and told everybody, "This is what this means. This is how we make it work for us."

It wasn't a threat, like, "You need to meet this timetable, or you'll never build anything bigger than a doghouse in Texas again." They knew how the project was supposed to go before they started to work. Once they were using it properly, they came to understand the value of a well-planned schedule.

"All we've got to do is make sure we have these quantities of these materials on this spot on this day with this many people, and we use that stuff to do this much work."

They weren't doing it, at first. So, we helped them do it until they understood it well enough to do it all on their own. They became intimately acquainted with all the details, including how their work affected other peoples' work, and how others' work affected theirs. That's when they started doing things I would never have imagined they could do. Everyone began taking the initiative, morale went sky-high, and work proceeded efficiently.

It didn't happen overnight, of course. I think it took about six months before we saw any real changes in behavior—the beginnings of our new culture. This book is about alignment, about getting everybody on the same page and keeping them there. Such alignment takes a while, especially when it's never been standard practice among the people on the project.

I think it took a full year to get everybody truly on the same page. We could've established the rapport from day one and saved a whole year, but construction was, and still is, mostly a team-against-team industry. Changing minds is a slow process.

I developed a lot of respect for the people at the Texas Department of Transportation. They're mostly engineers, very smart people who don't get paid the kind of money they'd get working in the private sector. They're very proud of what they do. They understood how things were built, but didn't understand the timing and relationship between all the factors on projects, so problems arose that they didn't have the tools to resolve. If you were the owner and a contractor came up to you with a problem, you could say, "That's your problem. Fix it." Everything would stop until the contractor figured out a solution.

On this project, identifying and solving problems became everyone's responsibility. Once, we had a TxDOT guy say, "You know, you poured that foundation wrong. You need to rip it out, let's do it again." It wasn't said condescendingly or punitively; it was, "Something's wrong, and you've got to fix it."

The contractor responded, "Okay, how about we do this and this?"

"Yes, that'll work."

It's a courteous and professional discussion, not "I'm the boss, and you're going to do what I say."

We started a new era in Texas road work. We made a few mistakes and adjustments, but eventually got our collective act together. That first year was hard, and we weren't as successful as we could've been, but using those first-year lessons, we improved enough so that the work in later years made up for it.

## Making It Happen

I had spent the first year on the project mostly by myself, researching potential roadblocks and setting the goals for this project. I'd promised the people that I worked for that we could build this in three years, and we wouldn't get to use the transit way until the whole thing was done, so there was an incentive to make that happen. TxDOT was sure it would take six to seven years, but if I could do it in the three I insisted on, we'd save vast amounts of taxpayer dollars and the people of Houston would have new bus routes in operation years before the state thought it could happen.

That's why I spent a year proving it and getting everybody aligned. Honestly, as I think back on it, it's all sort of cloudy, but I remember that I did nothing but research and plan the system and put together documents that showed everybody how it needed to be done. I took the plan to AGC because I knew I'd need their support. They said, "Yeah, this guy is right. We don't see anything wrong with what he's trying to do. This can work." With that kind of support, TxDOT said, "Okay, let's go for it."

Houston Metro, my employer, was impressed we got them to commit to that and probably a little surprised. The contracts were issued with my schedule, and we managed the project with them.

That first year was about building team alignment, confidence, and trust. The contractors needed real-world experience in this new way of thinking and doing before they felt secure in their ability to cut the project timeline in half. By the end of that year, the attitude was, "Hey, they're doing what they say they would do, so can we." Everybody started getting things done better, and what they once thought was an unrealistic timeline became the normal pace. They knew what they were going to do every day–they were going to pour this much concrete, and they needed this many people on site to do it.

This culture was especially important in navigating the interface points between the project's four segments. Each segment had been contracted to a different firm, meaning there'd be an interface between segments one and two, two and three, and three and four. This could've been a big problem in a competitive culture -- one that didn't care about how the work of one team might impact another -- but it wasn't a problem for us. The contractors started helping each other get things done quickly and correctly. They actually started getting out of their comfort zone and saying stuff like, "You need some extra help with that concrete? I'll be right over."

When they realized that helping each other benefited them all--that it was not about them but about the project--the change in the atmosphere on the project was something I'd never experienced before. I'd never seen that kind of cooperation and collaboration between four construction companies on a major project. Even TxDOT saw the culture that had come together, and they came along. No competition, just collaboration. That was a highlight of my career.

At the end of the job, they all got together and gave me a framed poster. It actually made me cry. It was such a significant professional moment for me. It said to me, "We won, all of us!"

The concept of CM Neutral was born on this project.

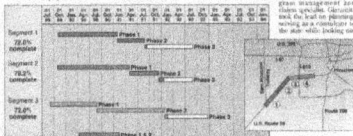

# CHAPTER 3

# An Ivy League Institution in New York (Late 1990s)

*I want to dedicate this chapter to Mark Burstein, Patricia Lancaster, Charlie Maikish, Anne St. Mauro, Joseph Mannino, and Steve Smolinski. They allowed and contributed to this staff's development into a team that completed every project on time, on budget, and to the expectations of our academic clients.*

## The Basics

### The Team

While working as an independent consultant in 1996, I was asked to join the design and construction department of an Ivy League university as Project Director, overseeing projects for the university's various professional schools. When I was brought on, the department had fifteen people on staff, several active projects, and a budget of over $100 million. The business, engineering, and law schools were the most active fundraisers, and their steady flow of capital meant that they were my primary focus for much of my time on campus.

By 1998, the department had grown into a very diverse group of civil, mechanical, and structural engineers, architects, project managers, schedulers, and administrative support. Altogether, we had about two dozen staff, two-thirds of whom worked on my portfolio, reporting directly to me--theoretically, they all worked under me but on projects overseen by other directors. This was *The Dirty Dozen* times two: each staff member came from different backgrounds, experiences, and cultures.

After about a year and a half, it became clear that the speed of the team's growth and the volume of project work had created a status quo that couldn't continue. They weren't cooperatively a team. Half of them worked on projects I oversaw, the other half for another director on other projects. I didn't have full control over what they did, but I could influence the way they acted, which inspired me to build a new team mentality.

Back in those pre-pandemic days, we gathered the technical team every week for a staff meeting in our office located in a nice brownstone near campus. With everyone in attendance, we discussed status updates on each of our projects. As I sat there one day, I thought how interesting it was that we were having major problems even with a team that had people with such great and varied experiences. I said, "Listen, today I want everybody to go around the room, and tell us about your experience. Explain what you do really well, and what you suck at." Everybody took a turn of five minutes or so explaining their expertise and how they could help other team members when someone ran into a problem in their area. Some of it was just egos talking (to be expected), but most were accurate--we were a truly talented group.

This introduced a foundational element I gleaned from the TxDOT project that would later help define "One Team. Shared Success.": know what your people do best and get them to do it.

The next meeting went differently. When somebody brought up a problem, I asked, "Well, did you call this person, the one with experience with this sort of thing?"

The answer was, unsurprisingly, "Well, no." I'd introduced a new way of thinking, but based on my experience with the highway project, I knew it would take time to catch on. I asked, "Well, why didn't you?"

Silence. No one had a good reason why they didn't or couldn't; it simply had not occurred to anyone.

This marked the beginning shift of our approach and methodology. We ran through this exercise several times. Each time, it brought together those with complementing strengths and weaknesses. In a very short time, everyone ceased to be embarrassed about asking for help, resulting in seamless problem solving and enhanced collaboration.

Every week when we met, we would discuss the schedule running on early start dates. When my team missed those, they knew I would ask them to explain what happened. If the answer was, "Well, I didn't know how to do that, but John knew and helped us through it," they knew the conversation was going to end on a positive note. We might have missed the start date, but they were working together to get back on track.

If there was a problem, they knew how to call the person who could solve it. We all knew who could help and how, because we'd discussed it. We recorded it all, put it on paper, and distributed it to every team member. Now, we simply needed to make that practice a habit.

Part of this culture change required that each team member look beyond their own projects to a greater, collective goal -- even if they reported to different stakeholders.

I spent another year dedicated to creating a cohesive, effective team with the goal of facilitating greater collaboration. I wanted everybody to be successful. For example, one of my senior project managers (SPM) and I were talking one day, and I asked how this SPM's project was going.

I was told, "It's going great."

I then asked, "Well, how is that other PM's project going?"

"Not so well. That project is behind schedule."

I hit my SPM with the new attitude I was trying to implement. "Well, what did you do to help? Did you do anything?"

"No," was the reply. My SPM was probably thinking, *of course not. This project is my project, and that project is that PM's project, not mine.*

I said, "Okay, but if that PM fails, you also fail, I fail, and we fail as a team." The SPM looked at me quizzically as I continued, "Let's go out there and figure out what's going on." So, out we went. The problem? The team was unorganized, and the sequence of work was a little out of whack.

The PM worked for my company, but was reporting directly to a university director, which created a level of disconnect in terms of approvals and priorities. Due to the schools' schedule, most of our work had to be done during the summer when fewer staff and students were on campus. Sometimes we did a classroom renovation, while other times, the whole floor of a dorm needed a makeover. Despite the size, budget, and scope of a project, we always had ten weeks, so everything was very fast-paced—it's a lot to put in place and keep on schedule.

The SPM and I closely reviewed the project with the PM. We figured out what was wrong and passed on our advice, presenting it to the project team in one of their meetings. Everybody agreed, after they tweaked it a little bit, that our proposed solution was the way to go. The PM took it from there, and the project finished successfully.

That SPM and I are still very good friends. We got together recently, and my old friend said, "Mike, I remember when you told me that everybody's got to win. If one doesn't win, we all don't win, and we lose as a team." His mention of the memory showed the impact of my disrupting the status quo. They got it, they bought it, and they did it. Those years were a great run, and the team was phenomenal.

We succeed as a team. We fail as a team.

This experience taught me a lot about how to build a team—this was the first time I'd built one like this—and we learned a few lessons the hard way.

I have always felt that everyone deserves a chance to be a part of the team. When I started in this business, I made a decision to not be the person that comes in and immediately cleans house. I was not going to fire anybody; I was going to work with them until we got it right. Termination, in my mind, is the easy way out--the better way to get involved is by getting people to work together.

An administrative assistant walked into my office one day and said, "I'm not working with that person anymore." Rather than looking for the root of the problem, they'd made the decision to stop communicating entirely, which was one day going to have consequences for the rest of the team. I replied, "Well, then, I guess you have to leave our team, because that person's part of the team."

The administrative assistant found a way. They changed their reaction -- their behavior -- and created the culture I was encouraging independently.

That turned into the best team I--or shall I say, we--have ever built and managed. I drove the process, but it would never have worked unless the team members joined in and made it work. Some teams thrive because they find a common ground to latch onto, but this one did not. We brought together many different types of people—from literally all over the world—to create a truly diverse talent pool that learned to rely on each other.

It doesn't just happen; over time, through team building, they changed the way they did things.

One day, I walked into the conference room, poured myself a cup of coffee, and watched everybody asking everybody else, "How can I help?", "So can I help you with something?"

These were the right kind of conversations, ones in which they were all engaged with each other's projects and invested in one another's success. I just turned to them, and said, "Okay, team, done. We're there, folks. Keep it going. Meeting over for today, go out and have fun!"

We did, in fact, have a lot of fun working with the university. It was often challenging; the school is universally acknowledged as one of the top institutions of higher learning in the world. When you work with them, you work with very smart deans and directors who expect delivery of the best quality.

Happy teams complete great projects with even greater results.

## The Details

### No Guilt, No Trespassing

As I was working to build team spirit, I asked myself, "How do I relate this new idea to other team members without creating any sense of guilt or pain?" Imagine that you're one of my PMs. I come to you and say, "Look, I understand that you're ahead with your project, but this is a team effort, and another PM is way behind."

If not communicated correctly, it can come across as "I'm blaming you or holding you responsible for some other person's lack of progress or success." That is *never* what a leader does. I talk about the team in terms of the old Musketeers' slogan, "All for one and one for all!"[9]

It's not just that you're sacrificing yourself in some way for others. In the formative stages of the new *modus operandi*, I didn't expect everybody to have the new way internalized—I never tried to make anyone feel guilty because they hadn't thought to work together this way; we were forming new habits, and we were still in the education phase.

---

[9] Alexandre Dumas, in collaboration with Auguste Maquet, *The Three Musketeers*, first serialized in Le Siècle, March to July, 1844.

As leaders, the goal is to set an example. I jumped in personally, both the SPM and I went over there, and we figured out what was wrong with the project. We operated behind the scenes, showing the PM a way to fix what had gone awry. The PM was having a problem organizing the people because the plan was not workable, so I suggested the approach we would use. We did this without the participation of the university employee supervising that project, and therefore, we also had to do it in a way that respected the university's position. We remained strictly in consulting mode. A week later, the PM walked into his university manager's office and said, "You know, I was looking at stuff with another project manager at my firm. We talked and looked at some problems I was having, and I decided to reschedule the whole project. This is what I did, and I'm sure it'll be successful." The university director liked it, gave the go-ahead, and they brought the project in on time.

## No Pride, No Ego

You will come across pride sometimes. Not the professional pride that demands you do your best every day, but egotistic pride. When you're working with someone who's particularly talented at their job, they might also be something of a lone wolf operator. How do you bring them effectively into the team? Can you convince them to sacrifice their pride for the rest of their peers?

As a last resort, you can always remove those people, but I prefer to help change their approach if possible. Our team adopts the idea that we sacrifice ourselves a little for others. Wouldn't that also apply to putting effort into helping a team member with a personal or attitude problem correct that flaw? If some new technology comes along, companies will spend the time and money to train people on how to work with it because it's in its best, long-term interest to add to their skill set--so why not show that same level of investment in interpersonal optimization?

In that same vein, this team isn't the only one we'll join. When a project ends and the team members move on to other endeavors, you want the experience on your project to make them better than when they started, and they will be if they're truly converted. That reflects well on you as the former supervisor and your company as a whole, as it's simply a case of good mentoring.

Egotism isn't part of our corporate culture. No team should accept that nonsense ever. When people try to control others or run roughshod over others' opinions, they need to be counseled—privately, politely, and clearly:

"This is the way this team operates. You have your place, they have theirs. No one steps on other people's toes. No one considers themselves above anyone else. We each contribute our best, and we all value each other's contributions."

If the lone wolf is a mature, professional adult, they grow out of this attitude. You get a win when you don't have to remove someone because they're in the way. You get a win when a problem person learns the value and power of synergy—that old notion that the whole is greater than the sum of the parts. When someone comes to understand that, and most do, it frees everybody up, takes the handcuffs off, and amazing things happen. If not, well, the decision to let them go is theirs.

There are other aspects to pride:

- Being unwilling to listen to people who are "beneath you"
- Becoming defensive when problems arise

- Focusing on fixing blame (away from yourself, of course) rather than solving the problem

Anyone can be guilty of these attitudes, and most of us are or have been at least once or twice. By being open-minded, solutions can arise from surprising places, and my experience with this Ivy League institution illustrated that on several occasions.

We began planning, designing, and constructing the new business law building in 1998. In total, the university spent about $50 million on this building, but most importantly, it was the first on campus to be equipped with electronic voice and video recording in every classroom. In all respects, this was a very big deal, so the project came under the direct oversight of the dean, with whom I became very close as a result.

Everybody knows problems arise and mistakes get made. The key is how you handle them. We got to the point where we were nearly closing up—installing the audio-visual equipment. In this case, the problem was a two-inch cable conduit. We had to fit a four-inch cable into that two-inch conduit. I repeat—building inspectors can make exceptions, but Sir Isaac Newton can't be bribed.

Those cables needed to run between the podium in the middle of the room to the AV control room on the side, about a hundred feet altogether, and we didn't have enough space for the wiring. The day after we discovered this problem, the contractor showed up with jackhammers out, ready to move furniture and rip up the carpet and floor.

Here was the worst-case scenario—destroying work done properly to repair work done improperly. I put my foot down and said no. I'd been trying to instill teamwork in my people for a year and I needed a team solution. I called the contractor's whole crew into a room, where we sat for about an hour.

Some people went into that meeting asking, "Are you blaming me for something?"

I replied, "No, I'm not blaming you. We have a problem. What you did resulted in this problem, but it's done. Now, we need to move on to solving this problem, and I don't care who comes up with the fix. I'm not tearing this building up. How do we get a four-inch cable through a two-inch conduit? That's all I want you to think about."

Level the playing field among the team members.

The point is the solution, not who caused the problem, nor who found the solution.

About forty-five minutes into this conversation, a twenty-five-year-old AV tech–you know, the youngster in jeans and a tee shirt–spoke up:

"Mike, I think I may have a solution. Last year, we did a project, and it was not the same problem, but we were trying to get twice as much throughput on a cable, and we found a little device we bought for like twenty-five dollars or fifty dollars, and it worked."

We could've said, "Shut up, kid, let the grown-ups talk," (That's ego talking, in case you missed it), but we didn't. We said, "Okay, so, we have a four-inch cable and a two-inch conduit. Let's try it." For less than five hundred dollars, we solved this problem in fourteen electronic classrooms instead of possibly spending upwards of $2 to 3 million to completely rip apart and rebuild, which certainly would've delayed the building's opening.

That would've been a disaster! The dean personally oversaw this project because a new executive program was scheduled to start just weeks after the anticipated reopening date in 1999. That program, in case you're interested, is now world-famous. Faculty, administrators, students, and everybody else were waiting on us so they could get started. The dean couldn't miss that day, meaning we couldn't. Imagine the damage to our reputation that would have resulted -- if we hadn't been open-minded about where the solution could come from.

Was it a great solution? It worked.

Stop, think, grab the team, and figure it out—and if it's the apprentice instead of the senior project engineer who comes up with a viable fix, don't let your ego get in the way of following the advice! Give that youngster a bonus.

You don't have to be the one who comes up with the solution. If you help get to a solution, you've contributed to the win. Maybe the tech's idea wouldn't have worked the way it had on that previous project, but maybe that idea would have inspired someone else with an approach that did work. That's a big part of building the team synergy, getting people to speak up and voice their opinions--and getting them comfortable enough to do it, because they know you aren't going to immediately shoot them down. When you get everybody together on the same playing field and focus on the challenge, great things happen.

I left the university after four years, armed with new approaches and ideas that I'd take with me to my next project. About a year later, I heard the school wound our Team down to zero. There'd been some organizational challenges, like accounting—two dozen people invoicing their time each week was not fun for the school. Some of the people from my team were invited to join the university's facilities office because every job we did for them was a success. We built solid relationships with the deans and, in fact, all the school personnel. They would say, "No, we want those guys doing our work, not the in-house people." That was the start of the end, right? Why hire consultants when you have an in-house team? Why not bring the consultants onto the team? The opportunity to better integrate, rather than dissolve, was there, but times change, and we must change with them. One thing is certain in my mind: when I left, my team members were better professionals than when we got together, and so was I.

We renovated ourselves while we renovated those old ivy-covered halls.

# CHAPTER 4

# A Major Airline at an International Airport in New York (Mid to Late 2000s)

*I want to dedicate this chapter to Farid Cardozo, Simon James, and Palmina Teta Whelan. We learned so much from each other as we changed the path forward–forever.*

## Change Orders

We were asked to take over as program manager for the construction of a new airline terminal that would total more than 1.5 million square feet. The project had been underway for several years with another program manager, so we weren't quite sure what we were going to find, but I knew what we could do.

Airports and airlines are notorious for change orders, because the architects, engineers, and contractors interface primarily with the executives and government agencies responsible for building the project -- no different than the Texas highway expansion -- rather than the people who would ultimately operate the facility on a day-to-day basis. When the terminal was built, the operators didn't hesitate to call out their issues with it.

"I don't like the carpet. I don't like the windows. I don't like this. I don't like that."

When we came onto the scene, the previous program manager had not left yet, so I asked, "How many change orders do we have?"

"Oh, we don't have any."

"No, that's impossible."

"Well, I've got a box under my desk where I've been collecting stuff."

"Okay. Get the box out."

Unsurprisingly, we found a couple of hundred change orders in that box. Everyone had just been ignoring them. I put one member of my team in charge of overseeing the change orders and another to handle scheduling--which we later found had its own challenges.

As part of the process of negotiating the pile of change orders, the contractor had sent out numerous requests for information (RFIs) that we needed to answer. Most of them were along the lines of, "There's a problem. Give us a price to fix that problem." The contractor's estimator would then price the change order. That price then went up the line to the owner to review, where we'd look at it and then send it back.

When the contractor or the construction manager is reviewing the changes, they're not doing it from the perspective of the trades. They're reviewing the changes to make sure they've got enough money in the budget to cover them. The change orders and RFIs go up and down, back and forth being negotiated endlessly. None of the issues were actually getting resolved.

Separately, we noticed the contractor had excessive general conditions costs, including people that were driving from New Jersey to the airport, which was on the opposite side of New York City. These operating costs were not only unnecessary but spoke to the mentality of their team and whose interests they had in mind.

I came up with an idea to address these inefficiencies. We were not sitting face-to-face with the people responsible for the terms of the change orders and were wasting huge amounts of time going back and forth. We needed to go directly to the source.

This setup was, so far as I knew, an original idea. I don't know of any project where anybody had removed the contractor's estimators for negotiations. We convinced the airline to let us do it, and we worked through every change directly with each of the trades. The contractor was invited to attend, but my team led the negotiations.

The process ultimately saved the airline $80 million without a battle. Those savings, in large measure, were due to the trades. They bought into this new idea because we offered them a different deal: If we negotiate this change order and put it into a record, it gets paid in thirty days. There was no BS; they got it done, and we got them paid.

This model was not at all the norm. Change orders in construction are supposed to start with an "entitlement" review, but that rarely happens. "Entitlement" means that the owner has changed the work--either modified in, added to, or deleted from their contract--in a way that changes the price. Money is then owed to the contractor or credited back to the owner. Often, changes come with an added cost attached—so the trade is entitled to more money, because of that change. Moving a wall that was already installed, for example, is entitled. Some changes can be implemented in the field without added cost. Moving the position of a wall that hasn't been installed yet, for example, may not incur an increased cost. If it's determined that you have an entitlement, the trade then has to justify the scope and price of that change before implementation.

Many of the trades I've encountered in my career come up with a number, send that number over the fence to the general contractor or owner, and it goes back and forth and back and forth until everybody's satisfied. There's no real structure to this whole negotiation system. By being disciplined about what I wanted in entitlements, for us and others, we got through the process more quickly and to a more satisfactory conclusion.

Among our refinements to the process, we expanded the negotiation team. There are many reasons that justify change order requests, such as changed work, schedule acceleration, or an error or omission, to name a few. Our team wanted to recognize those possibilities, as they could affect the final cost of the change or the decision on entitlement, so we included everyone that we felt needed to be involved: the CM, the architect, the airline – anyone that may have caused or will be impacted by a change.

Everybody, then, was aware of what happened, why changes were made, what entitlements were agreed, and where all the money went.

Knowledge is power, and we empowered them to better control whatever part of the project they were contracted to do.

## Scheduling

Transparency, we learned, would also resolve many of the challenges with the project schedule.

In a typical scenario, the CM and the contractor prepare and/or update the schedule and submit it for the owners' approval. The owner reviews it and sends it back with comments or corrections.

Then it may go back and forth for thirty or sixty days after the date the work was performed. What you're left with is a historical report that does not allow proactive management of the project.

While we were digging into the backlog of change orders for the new terminal, my team also took over preparing and updating the construction schedule on a weekly basis. We used it as the agenda for the weekly project meeting—progress made, activities that fell behind, issues or possible delays, deliveries, RFIs, manpower requirements, etc. The entire team had complete visibility of where the project was and where it was going. Risks were mitigated, and many delays were avoided. We also introduced starting activities based on early start dates, similar to our approach to the Ivy League institution's projects.

Critical path method (CPM) schedules show four dates for each activity (except critical path activities): the early start and finish dates, and the late start and finish dates. The days between the early dates and late dates are called "float." If the float is equal to "0," the activity is considered critical -- number one priority, cannot be late -- and only shows two dates, start and finish. My philosophy is if you start early, you finish early. You are constantly de-risking the project, as activities are completed, and there is less work moving forward. The benefits to the trades are that they actually make more money earlier in the process. They can better plan their manpower, equipment, deliveries, logistics, etc. It is a win-win for everyone. See the example, Early versus Late Dates, that illustrates executing activities on the early start dates resulted in saving sixteen months, effectively de-risking the schedule.

Float is not your friend, but *early dates* are. The early date schedule is the perfect schedule. Trade flow, manpower, deliveries, and successor activities are optimized. When I rallied the team around the early date deadlines, I believe this was the first time anyone flipped these roles and created success for everyone involved. Every project I perform, I bring this mindset and these processes, and we experience greater success for all parties.

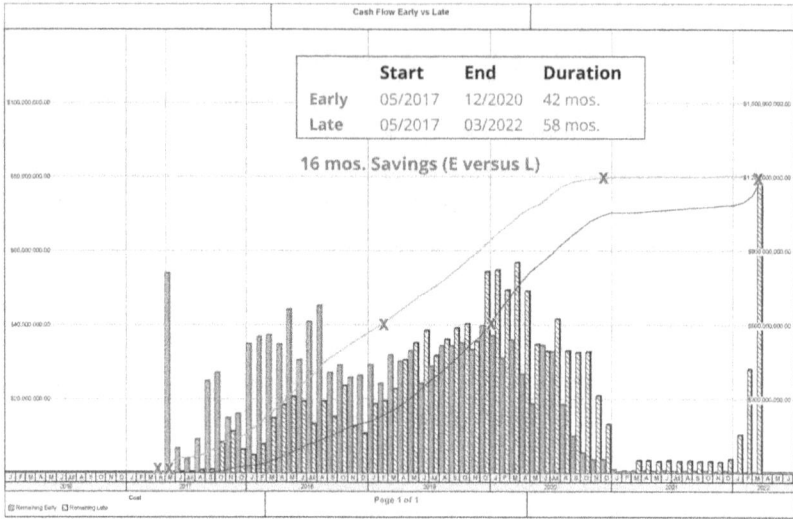

Example of Early versus Late Dates

# CHAPTER 5

# A Global Financial Institution in Washington, DC (2017 to 2019)

*I want to dedicate this chapter to Chris Hemus, Zeyad Ali, Greg Ferguson, Tommy and Frank, Andrew Sleth, Chip Scott, Michael Zetlin (Esq.) and the client staff, tradesmen/trade contractors. We went through the culture gauntlet together to accomplish the impossible.*

*CM Neutral concepts allowed us to start but not complete, and One Team. Shared Success.*sm *was born.*

## The Call

In 2016, I had breakfast with the business development lead for a construction company in New York City to share what Group PMX was all about. Among other things, I mentioned we had begun developing a process for how we do business, which, at that time, we called, "CM Neutral."

"What is it?"

"Well, it's about relationships—about trying to improve project performance by removing obstacles that get in the way on most projects."

"Well, let me see the sell sheet."

A "sell sheet" is a one-page outline of what we offer. I sent it out and got the response:

"This intrigues me. I know a project in another city that's having all kinds of problems. I'm going to send this to my friend down there."

Everybody knows how those things go; that was the last time I expected to hear about it. A little more than a year had passed when I got a call from the Corporate Services Facilities Director (CSFD) for a Global Financial Institution.

"Mike, I got your sell sheet from one of the guys here. I got it around a year ago, and I think I need your help. Can you come down?"

I said yes and flew out to meet with the CSFD. First, I met a lawyer at the door who had a nondisclosure agreement for me to sign. As the CSFD later explained the situation, I began to understand why that nondisclosure might have come into play. The renovation of the Global Financial Institution's HQ1 office building was not going according to plan. The project was originally envisioned as a four-year overhaul with a budget of $280 million. After four years of work, they were only approximately 50 percent complete, and the budget had ballooned to $360 million. They had a completion date of June 2017—not far off from that first meeting—but the building was only half done and was already estimated at $130 million over budget.

The CSF had one essential question: "What can you do for me?"

I replied, "Well, I don't really know what the underlying problem is." At that point, I'd only met with one person, so I didn't have the full picture of the situation we were dealing with yet.

"Why don't you come back with your team, and we'll sit down and discuss it?"

I also didn't have a team at that moment, so I quickly brought a group of good people together. We went down to sit in on one of the project meetings and get a better understanding of the dynamic. We quickly learned that yes, they were behind schedule and over budget, but *that* wasn't the underlying problem. The project team simply had no intention of or interest in working together -- from an outsider's perspective, it looked like everyone in the room hated everyone else. Or at least that's how the culture had developed over time.

That's when I learned the delays and budget issues were just the effects; the management team's approach was the root cause.

I'm sure you can picture it -- at that point, all politeness had gone out the window in favor of dodging blame and pointing fingers, including a few middle ones, creating an environment with more curse words than conversation.

When problems came up, the attitude was, "I don't care about that, that's their problem," or "That's the CM's problem, not my problem," leading to difficulties and roadblocks every step of the way.

There are punch list items -- or errors that need correcting -- at the end of every construction project. The contractor says they're done, but they weren't done right -- not installed properly or to the proper, specified finish level, etc. When we first became involved with this building, the first floor we looked at had a seven-thousand-entry punch list -- for that one floor alone! It was evident that the important QA/QC step was simply not happening. Additionally, there were nonconforming reports (NCRs) in abundance. These are more serious than below-par work typical of punch lists, as these describe work that didn't conform to the contract. In total, the first phase of the project had a forty-thousand-entry punch list in backlog, and the space was now occupied, making it that much more challenging to address.

All of this needed correction from a construction management perspective.

Simultaneously, the Global Financial Institution had leased several floors of a nearby, off-campus building for workers being displaced by construction. This meant they were spending a considerable amount of money on swing space, in addition to the costs of moving those workers back-and-forth, while their actual building project experienced fee-laden delays. Every step of the process overlapped into the next as the delays mounted, meaning each one took two to three times longer than it should've because everyone was working toward a different, unknown, and unshared goal.

The DF asked me, "Do you think you can fix this?"

"This" was hard to believe. I sat through that first meeting thinking this just can't be happening. Everyone was cursing at each other. F– your mother! F– your father! F– everyone! Both women and men were equally represented. The CM's PEx, who was running the meeting, was wearing a baseball cap with the letters "FU." He said it meant Florida University. I had tried to be honest with the people in that room. I told them, "Listen, I'm from New York, and I am offended by your talk and actions. I've never seen anything like this. Total disrespect for each other. Ugly, ugly, ugly."

They kind of laughed at me, so when the CSFD asked if I could fix it, I told him the problem is everyone hates each other. I explained what I laid out at the outset of this book: It's your team that gets you from the empty lot to the finished building. Without that team, without every individual member of it doing their jobs right, it doesn't happen—no dreams, no visions, no impact.

"What do you think you can do? Can you bring this team back? Where do we start?"

I asked about the range of my authority. The CSFD told me I had full authority, including removing any individual from the team, even the Financial Institution's own employees, if necessary. Authority and some degree of autonomy is key in a turnaround strategy, and while I didn't intend to remove anyone without giving them a chance first, it was critical that we had the approval to do so.

The CSFD also did not want me to remove any companies or trade contractors, A/E, or any other company participating in the reconstruction. I gave my word that we would not, unless they refused to change their attitudes, and we signed a contract to move forward.

From there, we requested that the contractor execute a rider contract to allow us to communicate with the trades directly. It was a carefully written, specific contract put together for me by a construction and claims lawyer who drew up the document pro bono, because it was such a new (meaning "disruptive") idea. When I asked why I wasn't being charged, the counselor responded, "I'm kind of interested in what you're trying to do."

At that time, you weren't allowed to talk to the trade contractors. It was simply one of the rules: you can't interfere with the means or methods. By talking to the trades, they thought you were interfering. This was the way it is on all projects.

Armed with the new contract, we said to their trades, "Here are the new rules that we're going to abide by from here on out. We want to observe what you all are doing to see if we can figure out where things are falling off the track and how we can do things properly moving forward."

The first trade contractor I met agreed to it, and it changed their lives. It changed everything about how we did business. The contractors got value from our new approach, inspiring it to become a part of the standard contract we present to the construction contractor.

We set the tone from day one that we're the project manager, and we want to be able to do this and that. If they agree, we all get a successful outcome.

During my first month on-site, I attended one of the Financial Institution's Board Meetings. The CFO asked me what I was going to do to turn this project around. I explained that our approach is aimed at identifying and removing obstacles every day that construction continues. Two of my team members, Tommy and Frank, were retired Supers who knew how to build and when things were veering off track. I told the CFO that they presented issues every day, and we resolved them every day. That was the last time I heard from the CFO.

## The Job

Mending broken or strained relationships in any business is difficult work.

That was our challenge: How do we get the people to work with each other and create that team atmosphere? How do we get all the people who were supposed to work with each other to actually do that instead of screaming at one another? Our work was definitely cut out for us.

New systems and processes can be one way of aligning people differently, because they aren't personal. Our process became the new formula.

I hired a thirty-year veteran of successful interior construction projects as my partner to provide additional interior construction expertise. We had three or four people on the ground at the job site every day, and the partners flew in weekly to shepherd people through our process.

It wasn't seamless. It took six months to get everyone on the same page, and not everyone made it there.

The Financial Institution had assigned its HQ1 Renewal Director of Facilities (RDF) to work with the construction company's chief operating officer (COO). We quickly found out that these two people in particular had a strained working relationship, making it next to impossible to facilitate any sort of collaboration. We started looking for common ground elsewhere. Whom could we get to come to the table first willing to bury the hatchet somewhere other than in the other person's skull? Our people were injected into the process, so we were to work with everybody. My management team became the common thread of cooperation.

I kept trying to get the RDF and the COO into the same room to start talking to each other—to start jointly planning actions to get the job straightened out. They refused.

In addition to those two, there was the contractor's project executive (PEx), who you may remember as the guy in the "FU" baseball cap. He wouldn't let anybody on the contractor's team talk without his personal nod. The PEx had to control everything going on. It came to a point that in one meeting that PEx nearly got into a fistfight with one of the Financial Institution's employees. I immediately called the COO, and the PEx was removed—no second chance. I just said, "No, it's over now. Please, do not let this person back on site."

I'll admit, the PEx had made his position known on day one, in that very first meeting we sat in on. We wanted to give everyone a chance to move forward with us, and it's important for building respect with the team that we did. We didn't come in to clean house, but we had to be realistic about behaviors that we didn't think would change.

Unfortunately, the PEx's removal wasn't the only change in personnel that took place. I sat down with the contracting company's president to go through their organizational chart a couple of times. I said, "This person is just not giving us what we need. I need somebody that can deliver in this area or that, but we aren't seeing the results we need." So, we started changing out people. It wasn't a mass firing. The president agreed with our feedback and assigned people that could perform in the areas we needed. Again, firing people wasn't the goal, but in some cases they'd chosen to be an obstacle, and I was being paid to remove obstacles.

"It's just business."

I say that now, but when we let the PEx go, the contracting company president wasn't happy. Well, one month later, the president came in and hugged me, saying, "Mike, you changed the atmosphere and culture of the job. The PEx was in our way, just about making money for himself. It wasn't productive."

The president saw the change. The environment flipped, over time, from being very negative to very positive. I do things for that purpose, and I don't look back. I knew what I had to do to get it done.

On another occasion, I delayed replacing someone, an employee of the Financial Institution. I had been given the authority to remove them, but in the end, I went to the Institution's CSFD -- the one that brought us on board to begin with -- and made the case that it was time for a change. The CSFD told me, "I've got this one. You're right, I've got to take that person off the project. I've got to do this."

After that, people really started to understand the behavior we expected. We knew we couldn't change behind-the-scenes behavior or animosity. We knew that if somebody wanted an excuse, there would always be some excuse to be found that would get in the way of real collaboration. If certain team members weren't doing it for the right reason, they didn't belong on the team. In those cases, you remove them from the team, and you set the new standard for what you expect on the job.

The RDF was the most drastic change I've ever had to make. Normally, people take the hint. They leave because they know the environment won't jive with their approach and they're unwilling to compromise. Others say, "I really like what's going on, so I'm going to stay and make it work." They adapt to the new status quo, and they end up enjoying coming to work.

> *The first element of our approach, CM Neutral, aligns people; it gets them talking to each other.*

I changed the organization of the project to make sure that communication was happening the right way. I restructured who worked together and restricted what they did. We divided the standard project management meeting into three different sessions:

1. The first, the commercial issues meeting, focused on contract changes, payments, and other foundational administrative matters.
2. The next, the delivery meeting, which was held at least every week, sometimes every day, focused on accurately assessing where we were presently. This ironed out scheduling issues between us and the contacting team. They looked at problems that could prevent on-time delivery and how to eliminate those problems. The schedule was the record of truth, every time, every day. The project adopted an early start date order.
3. The quality assurance and control meeting – QA/QC, though we didn't call it that back then – focused on working with the contractor at the trade level to educate them on best practices. Essentially, it's to say, "Do it this way, and we get a better result."

It took about six weeks before they started to walk into that room with the right approach unprompted, but it took those first six months to feel the change at scale. People began going out of their way to help each other out. In meetings, they became polite and respectful, partly, I'm sure, because we took action and removed people who weren't. The whole approach turned to focusing on how to remove problems, keep going, avoid delays, and prevent repetition. Conversations began to be like this:

- "We have a problem."
- "What's your problem?"
- "This is our problem."
- "Yeah, we know about that. We already got somebody working on that. They'll be in touch."

Or like this:

- "I have a problem."
- "Okay. How do we solve it?"
- "We need an architect in here" or "We need an engineer on this."

You cultivate the idea that problems get solved immediately. Everything's immediate. Not "Oh, we'll wait until next week to solve that problem." No, we resolve it today! As I said before, if you find out about a problem before noon, you have a chance to get it solved before the close of business that same day. If the solution arrives that day or the day after, progress resumes immediately. If solutions are stalled, you lose days or weeks of work in the schedule. Our job is to take the handcuffs off. Time constraints are in place for a reason, and when you remove obstacles as soon as you encounter them, you walk to that finish line instead of having to sprint.

> *This is the second element of CM Neutral -- focusing on fixing little things that quickly add up to savings in time, effort, and most importantly, money.*

The contractor and their team got used to working with us to resolve problems, but they soon learned that they could solve a lot of them without our help once they understood the process. They still depended on us to solve certain challenges – I was the interface between them and the Global Financial Institution, and it was my responsibility to remove the obstacles created by the client. The Institution had also stopped communicating internally, so issues on their side were never truly being resolved. Even their "quick fixes" weren't quick at that point. These issues, and their temporary band-aid solutions, only caused more delays and financial strain

We succeeded in resolving most of those problems and delivered three floors in just one year because everybody came around and adopted this more cohesive and collaborative approach. They were forced to get over any animosity and grudges. Organizationally, they changed their behavior. In fact, after we committed to the new process, there were hardly any changes requested for the project. Soon, we started hearing that the trades were talking about our team in a very positive way. "These people are working with us. They're really trying to help us. They're being independent. They're not just being the owner's advocate."

This was true; our mission was to advocate for the project. To us, there were no "sides," and the on-site people were beginning to see and respond to that approach.

Advocating for the project and eliminating adversarial relationships is the third element of CM Neutral.

Still, problems arose. We had overcome a lot but never expected a glass-smooth road to completion. I remember several instances of people asking to yell at someone who had done something incorrectly or created new challenges for the rest of the team.

"They need to know what went wrong so it doesn't happen again. A little yelling is due."

And then it was over, and everyone went back to business, because we had changed the culture on the job site. "It's not you, it's the problem." The team had earned one another's respect enough that they knew it wasn't personal. We weren't operating that way anymore.

That realization took time. I cannot emphasize enough that it took that whole six months of working together, and some "tough love," but we got them aligned. It became a lighter atmosphere that resulted in a successful project.

## The Seven Actions

Turning the Global Financial Institution's project around was one of the first true tests of the CM Neutral framework I was developing.

Getting the team aligned required us to remove people and relationships that weren't working for the benefit of the project, even though we didn't want to. When we rallied around the project, and ensured everyone on it did the same, things started to really come together. We weren't playing games or placing blame; we were making the work -- not anyone's egos -- the most important thing.

We were championing those three elements of the CM Neutral framework:

1.  Aligning people, getting them to talk to each other
2.  Fixing the little things that add up to savings in time, effort, and money
3.  Advocating for the project and eliminating adversarial relationships

As a leader, end goals are important. How to get there is another thing entirely. After the first meeting with the Institution's project team, I wrote down what I felt needed to happen to get there directionally. To get people aligned, you have to understand why they aren't aligned. You have to know the obstacle to remove it. In this case, the obstacle was part of the team itself, so getting rid of any bad blood went hand-in-hand with getting people to talk to each other.

What I wrote down after that first meeting were seven specific actions to turning the headquarters project around:

## 1. End Arrogance and Childishness

The first action must be — and I must make myself clear — to end any and all mean-spiritedness amongst the team. Before you can think about aligning people into a cohesive, effective team, you need to weed out any ugly arrogance. You cannot move forward with that in the culture. We got this point across early on by firing the general contractor's PEx. When someone comes in wearing a cap with bold letters "FU," they've crossed a line with a crude, unnecessary gesture that they can't cross back, no way, no how. While yes, some off-color commentary is tradionally present in the field, it cannot be accepted in the management team conference room. People in a professional setting shouldn't have to put up with any ounce of childish nonsense, and I won't permit it on any project I'm overseeing. So with that, we said a quick and final goodbye.

## 2. Staff Changes

Don't do it unless you must, but if you must, don't hesitate. A mean spirit is one thing, but people are either a good fit for the project and the team or they are not. People can do their job well, or they cannot. People can get along with others, or they cannot. I had to let go of two top-level people from the contractor's team. When I saw there was no adherence to the schedule, I fired the contractor's scheduler, and you already know what happened to the PEx. The Financial Institution's CSFD terminated his RDF, as he, along with the other individuals let go, insisted on standing in the way of positive progress.

## 3. Schedule Adherence

After releasing the contractor's scheduler, we implemented our proprietary scheduling protocol. We set it up, published it, and made everyone stick to it. Those schedules were rigorous and required us to meet with the on-site team every day to be sure they stayed on track. We never got mean or angry, but we also would not work on their schedule. We knew how long things needed to take, and those were the deadlines we would meet.

At one meeting, I let the contractor's team know, "We think you only need six weeks to finish the final punch list, FF&E, and customer experience on each floor."

He said, "No, no, we need twenty-four."

I said, "No, I'm giving you six, that's it. Here's the schedule, get your team together and figure it out." The contractor completed construction and obtained the temporary certificate of occupancy (TCO) before handing it over on the first date set in the schedule and every date after that, because we gave them a clear path to figure it out. Everyone had been putting Band-Aids on the problems, rather than resolving them. each challenge that arose. Every chance I had, I was ripping those Band-Aids off and driving, probably in some cases demanding, a solution. For the record, despite the accelerated schedule, customer satisfaction went up.

## 4. Alliance and Engagement

Nothing is independent; every activity relates to all the others -- especially in construction. Alliance and engagement involve several closely related processes: Getting the CM and every tradesman working together instead of sticking to their individual tasks and ignoring everything else. Nothing is independent; every activity relates to each other. Ensuring everybody on the project is advancing at the same time is critical, because a delay in any aspect means the possibility of more in other aspects. Getting people on the job site to engage with us is important so that when problems arise, they know who to call for help, and they know they'll get a solution. When this happens, there's a flow among the tradespeople that allows the contractor to manage work in detail.

## 5. Resolving Residual Bad Feelings

Bringing the designers back to the project to help resolve problems was not easy. There were a lot of hard feelings still burning hot, and they were hesitant to re-engage with the project team. I didn't blame them for their initial resistance, but we needed them. They knew the vision we were working to achieve, and their input on how it was being executed was essential. Fortunately, I was able to leverage some of my contacts to make it happen. Eventually, they realized that the culture had changed, and they completed the project on a very positive note, contributing much to its success.

## 6. Stay Neutral

When disputes arise, some people think that because you've heard them out, you agree with them by default. We got some interesting reactions the first time someone heard us say, "No, we're not siding with you unless you're right. So, if you want to submit a change order, it'd better be right, because if it's wrong, we're not going to pay for it. We're going to reject it." Allowing change order costs - right or wrong - to balloon at the Financial Institution's expense was a day-one problem we had already resolved, and we weren't going to let it repeat. When we first came on board, there was a claim against the Institution for about $50 million, and the contractor was understandably pushing for it to be settled. We negotiated, and in the end, we paid less than half for that claim. We got it settled because it was clear that we represented neither the contractor, nor the client. Our only intent was a settlement fair to both, and they signed an agreement that was equitable. We converted the contract from a GMP (Guaranteed Maximum Price) to a Lump Sum for the remainder of the work.

## 7. Get the Dollars Straight

Since the project was already over budget, only in part due to that claim, the numbers had to be reworked. The new budget considerations included extending the completion deadline for one year. It had been scheduled as a five-year contract, but we knew when we arrived that no one could finish in that time frame. We also had to tackle the top two floors, the executive suite, including a conference room and all the other trimmings suited to a top-tier organization. Naturally, we planned everything on those floors to be the highest level of finish, which was accounted for in the new budget. We also changed the contract from a guaranteed maximum price (GMP) to a lump sum project and settled the project price for good. Someone that was not the Institution was going to eat their mistakes from that point forward. In the end, the Institution's headquarters was completed under that final price tag.

## The Actions

Those are the seven specific actions I pulled out of our early review of the headquarters project. As I left that first meeting with the Institution's project team, they were just ideas – initial thoughts. Over time, they became necessary steps to the process. We sat down with everybody and showed them what our team intended to do and what problems we'd observed. Each problem got broken down into actionable items, and from there, we simply did what we knew would work. By this time, I'd been not only working on construction sites but turning them around for several decades. There were many things we knew to do simply because of experience. The rest of the crew got the vision and joined us. They had spent four years building the lower half. We finished the upper half following the CM Neutral framework in just two.

## The Difficulties of Implementation

You need to do what needs doing, and as I said, these steps are essential. But they don't happen in a vacuum, and as you've seen, they're not always easy. In fact, you should expect that pushbacks are almost guaranteed.

How do you keep the conversation - and the project - moving forward?

Do what needs doing.

When I first sat down with the contracting company's president to review their organizational chart, we were at dinner. It was the first time we'd ever met, but I brought the chart. It showed a large X over two or three people. The president looked at me and said, "Is this what I think it is?"

"Yeah, we need to replace those people."

"Is there a reason why?"

"Well, they're not performing to an acceptable standard, so they're not going to be part of the team that I'm putting together." Then I said, "The next thing is, we want to interview the people you're going to bring on board." I added, "I'm here to fix the problem. There are issues with members of your team *and* the Institution's. We're going to either convert them or remove them. It's very simple. I have no targets on anybody's back. I just want people who will do the right thing."

The president said, "Okay."

The interview with the Institution's CSFD went about the same in our first face-to-face meeting after we signed the contract. That chart had Xs through several boxes. As the CSFD looked at it, I said, "I guess you want to know what those Xs are, right?"

"Are they what I think they are?"

"Probably." I paused. "We want those people gone. I want to replace them with people that I know are going to benefit the project."

The CSFD said, "Okay, I'm on your side. Get it done."

These were serious, hard-point discussions, but never confrontational. I wouldn't go there, because I don't need to. Neither the Institution nor the contractor ever crossed that line either. The Institution was bleeding cash for this project, and they both knew it. They came to understand that I was fighting for the project, not for the contractor or the client. My team fought for both.

> *If we are honest and fair with each other, we can talk about any issue and resolve any problem like adults and professionals.*

Those key people gave me full autonomy to do whatever I felt needed to be done to get the project finished. Both knew that I didn't want to cross that line—to start a fight—because all of us knew that none of us would win. I think that both saw me as sincerely trying to be honest and fair, and they were the same with me.

## Alignment and Engagement

Bringing people back to the table wasn't as straightforward. Convincing the design team to re-engage with the project, for example, and tell the Institution, "Yes, we have problems, but we can solve them," wasn't easy. They would have to spend a lot of time and, therefore, a lot of money to solve some of those problems. That created the next discussion: what will you accept? What can we negotiate?

▎ *We negotiate honestly and openly.*

We were clear on the idea that we'd never use a lesser product, but we could use a different product or an alternative way of doing things to get the results we needed. It worked. Everybody was engaged in solving problems, which became a weekly, even a daily, thing. Over time, they all embraced the model. Our motto became, "We have a problem. Let's fix it and move on." We were understandably pleased to see this attitude arise. That's exactly what we hoped would happen with the implementation of CM Neutral.

## Get the Right People in the Job

On my second day, I interviewed the person in charge of scheduling and reviewed their credentials. What school had they attended?

"I went to the University of West Virginia, UVA."

"That's a good school. What did you get your degree in?"

She responded, "Civil engineering."

"What made you choose scheduling?"

"Oh, one of my parents recommended I go into it. My father."

"What does he do?

"He is a claims consultant."

Ironically, construction claims consulting was exactly what the scheduler was doing. I remind you of the definition: "A *claim* is a demand for something due or believed to be due…"[10]

The existing schedule was tied in knots. It wasn't a useful tool. It wasn't helping anybody get things done. That schedule existed to

---

[10]  Mirza, M. A. (2005) *Op. cit.*

show delays that the construction team experienced -- it was used as a weapon, just like I'd seen on the Texas highway project. In fact, that scheduler was put in place to cook those books — to make it look like everything was the Institution's fault, backing up data for that $50 million claim being built against the Institution. The scheduler has been doing this for years.

We sent them home, hired our own scheduler, and started using the schedule as a tool to move the project forward. We took their projected timeline, we rebuilt it, and then we put it back on the table as we announced, "Here's how we're managing the job going forward."

Did that cause blowback? No, not at all. There was a lot of talk on the jobsite, and that was probably a good thing. I didn't pay attention to it because it was a non-event; the scheduler was gone, and my team took over. The team then started doing our thing, and people started to line up and listen. They got the message that we had the authority to organize this team in the way needed to get the project done, which could mean getting rid of team members that couldn't get in line. While that was part of our contract, I've said before that we didn't go into the job planning on a mass firing. We really planned, well, hoped, to keep everyone if we could. We wanted those we had to let go of to change their attitudes and work together. These termination incidents did, in fact, change attitudes – about me. They gave me a different "place in line" there. In fact, when I fired the PEx, a lot of people on the contractor's side were relieved.

## Critical Path Method Scheduling

The critical path method (CPM) scheduling protocol called for a couple of things that are not usual in projects. In our CPM schedule, each activity had an early start and finish date, plus a late start and finish date. The difference between those two things is *flow*. We use this technique to avoid problems and delays.

*Start every activity on its early date, if possible.*

75

Do that and you don't stack tasks up, which is what invariably happens if a schedule isn't meticulously planned and forcefully carried out. We started telling the contractor, "You've got this activity that you can start today, so start it today."

"Oh, no, we don't need to do that. We've got this much flow."

I said, "No, we don't rely on the flow. Think about it. You're not taking advantage of the time you have today. If you start tomorrow, you've lost one day, and you will *never* make that day up. If you start today, you have a full extra day to find and solve problems without delaying later activities." So, they started adapting to our early start and early finish date protocols, and things started getting done on time. They started to see the benefit of never wasting a day.

This process was critical to our being able to finish construction on the top half of the Institution's building in half the time as the bottom. The top two floors I mentioned were the C-Suite. The finishes on those floors were all going to be extremely high end, the best work in the business. We needed to start planning those floors immediately, even though work wouldn't start on them for months, to ensure they were done to the correct standard.

So that's what we did. We created a schedule, lined up the tradesmen, and we got all the materials and finished them on time with the floors done just as planned.

We also had resource loading in the schedule. People met each day to review it, because that was their assignment. We had a program that captured the people, that is, checking the manpower we needed against the plan and the scheduled activities. Every day, we'd conclude that we had enough to get the scheduled work done or not enough people had shown up to complete the task. In that case, we'd call the contractor and say, "You need X number of additional people on site. We can use them."

Managing field resources was the whole purpose of that protocol. It enabled us to make sure enough workers were onsite to get the job done. It worked so well that we now use it on our other projects as a standard protocol.

## Sharing Resources and Changing Attitudes

Back in 2004, I had an older version of the process that eventually became CM Neutral. Even though this original package didn't have an organizational component, there was a measure of success with it. Through experiences like those I describe in this book, we refined and expanded the framework.

The whole philosophy of CM Neutral is about helping one another and sharing resources. Later on, I realized that while sharing resources was valuable, we could create a bigger and better benefit by changing behaviors and the way they worked fundamentally. Organizing the team differently allowed me to put the right people in the right places and get them focused where I wanted them—on delivery!

"Delivery" simply means getting things done, and we wanted to affect delivery by reducing delays. That part of the framework became much clearer during this project because I had the authority from the client to do whatever I needed to do to get their project done. I used that power to prove my theory that the process needed an organizational component, resulting in our ability to take that project to the next level.

I'd never done this before on this large of a scale, and it really allowed me to hone the skill. I'd agreed to fix a situation where I was without solutions on day one, but I had the framework. I knew what the end goal looked like, but I'd put myself in a situation where I didn't know how to get there. I came out of that first meeting thinking, "What do I do next?"

We stayed focused on identifying problems and developing a plan to solve them. When it started to work, I saw the impact it had on behavior and said to myself, "Wow, this is great, because the people are changing." The evolution of the CM Neutral framework, our new approach, "One Team. Shared Success." grew out of that.

The project team that moved forward was willing to collaborate. We had rebuilt a team of dysfunction into one where everybody cared and got things done by helping others to identify and solve problems.

## Objectives and Methods

The objective given to us by the Financial Institution on day one was simple: "Fix this thing. Get the building completed in time for its scheduled opening."

The Institution's headquarters were a more complex deal with bad behaviors at every turn than the projects I'd worked on up until that point, which challenged me and my team to take our game up a notch. We needed to create that behavior/cultural change.

When we started, I truly had no idea what I was doing. I could not see the *problems*, only the *symptoms* of the problems -- the schedule, the change orders, the resources. I didn't know initially if they were the actual causes of the delays, and figuring that out took some digging. As our involvement progressed, we started to see clearly where the real problem lay—we needed to affect a major change of heart in all the people involved. Had we not dug to get past the symptoms, we'd never have reached the people at the root of the problems.

So, I said, "Okay, I can do some things." I knew I could do the scheduling. I could do the change order negotiation. I could share resources. But because those things do not and cannot happen in a vacuum, inevitably I found myself taking over the whole project -- again.

My existing strengths in scheduling and negotiating created a measure of trust, a foundation. When the change orders came in, the Institution's leadership trusted us and what we were doing, because they could see tangible behavioral changes and successes. We opened and finished the first portion of the project on time, just like we said we would, along with every activity after that. As we finished each floor and moved all the furniture in, a core team member went around opening every door and turning on every light to make sure everything worked. When the person who would use that office went in and sat at that desk, we wanted to hear, "Yeah, my place works." That created client satisfaction that evolved into trust because it looked better, it felt better, and it worked.

One reason for this outcome is that I assigned both the project engineers and the project architects to the quality control and assurance team. Quality control -- ensuring the work being done is up to the standards of the client's quality assurance team -- is something the contractor usually handles. Nobody ever does it right that way.

Instead, I put the people who are normally on the client's quality assurance team -- those architects and engineers -- on the quality control team on the front end. Their job was to have a zero-item punch list. "I don't need to have a list of the same item replicated a hundred times in a hundred rooms because you guys didn't check it. From now on you are on Quality Control." This helped the team adjust their perspective. They were fixing problems *now* and preventing them from continuing, instead of pointing them out later.

They said, "You're right. Let's go into the first room and correct the way the trades are installing things because we know what it's supposed to look like. We're the architects, we're the engineers. A pipe's got to be finished exactly this way. The handle's got to be turned that way."

Every building has things that were drawn into the plans, but the trades took liberties and did it in whatever way they wanted to. By making sure things were completed correctly up front, we had fewer delays and a significantly shorter punch list.

It's like that old wise man said, "If you don't have time to do it right once, you sure as hell don't have time to do it twice." All these things improved the delivery.

All of this happened because our people's attitude became, "Let's turn over a great job to the client." They all bought into the project just as our team had, and they didn't want me to go review something and find a mistake or substandard work. They wanted to be proud of what they'd done. That became my objective early on, and that professional pride ultimately changed the whole process.

## Benefits

This approach was, to a degree, the culmination of the framework I'd been developing for years. For example, earlier in my career, on the highway project, I developed a system to track activities and make people collaborate. When I worked with the University, we did something similar. We created a team approach to building multiple projects, which became very successful through the multiple benefits it produced.

CM Neutral grew into more than just what I thought it could be in those early days. It became something with which I could organize an entire project to be successful every time, and that's what it's evolved into present-day. This process, as you've seen, comes with tremendous benefits.

*Cooperation*
The team changed from one where they battled with each other at every turn – a culture of constant conflict – to one that did whatever needed doing to get the job done. We developed the phrase "Project-First Thinking," which I continue to use to this day. Every subcontractor went in there with their company hat on, but in the end, they had no company hats, and they had the client's best interest in mind.

*Unity*
The schedule was developed by all the people involved to be the blueprint for all that we did. Having one schedule (instead of the two or three that most jobs have) became our "source of truth" and kept everything on track. The project was reconciled weekly. The schedule was cost- and resource-loaded, and those numbers were reviewed every week.

*Better Decisions*

We began making decisions based on factual data rather than gut reactions, gut feelings, or past experiences. It wasn't just, "Get the job done on time and under budget." We encouraged a *best practices* approach.

For example, we had a roofing issue. The original idea was a cold tar (also referred to as a high tar) roof, but that had some negatives for the people working in the building. We walked through all the different alternatives, but the client's representative remained adamant about what they wanted. So we met with that person privately and said, "Listen, I'm sorry, but this is a much better approach, and this is how we're going to do it. I've checked with the engineers. The high tar roof does have benefits, but those benefits don't outweigh the negatives."

The Institution came around after we demonstrated that we were right with solid science.

*Strong Personal Relationships*
I was in a meeting one time and reminded them that what we were doing had ramifications in the long term. "This is not a 'this-job-only' thing, people," I said to them, "You're all working for this so well, and you've cultivated strong, positive relationships with everybody. Those relationships should continue to grow and build even stronger personal ties." In this experience, the process was allowed to happen, coming together in ways that we didn't realize were possible before now. The team was empowered at every level. They made decisions that were in the best interest of the project, not selfish ones. If they work together in the future, there'll be trust and confidence that will allow them to start that next project in far better shape than when we started this one. They won't repeat past mistakes.

*Transportability*
The most important revelation that came to me during this entire process highlighted the idea that CM Neutral had grown into something that could work with any project - One Team. Shared Success. That was a huge eye-opener. It became a disruptive behavior – a change in some of the fundamentals of the industry. Back in the

day, people weren't doing it this way. This grew into something that allowed me to feel great about what the team did and how it changed the approaches of each person who brought the project to life. We had two to three hundred people on this job site every day. Eventually, all worked synergistically to transform a struggling project into a massively successful one. They saw what was going on, adopted the principles and practices we espoused, and used them to do something wonderful.

Can't ask for more, can we?

# CHAPTER 6

# Fortune 500 Airline at International Airport in New York City (Early 2013 to the Mid-2020s)

*I dedicate this chapter to Ryan Marzullo, George Guillaume, Steve Aspden, Simon James, and Anthony Manganiello. Without their support and hard work, these changes would have never come to life - One Team. Shared Success.* sm

I began my fifth major aviation project in 2013 when a carrier decided to renovate its existing terminal buildings at a large metropolitan airport. The initial budget was approximately $300 million for the refurbishment -- no expansion, just aesthetic improvements and fixes.

In 2017, the project grew to include a new, 1.5-million-square-foot terminal building, including four separate concourses (where you embark and disembark from planes), which would increase their presence and efficiency.

At that time, the airline had just under fifty gates. The new terminal wouldn't add additional gates, but it would vastly improve passenger and plane movement and efficiency on the airfield.

The Construction Management team was being led by another firm. We were asked to provide a prime contract for the construction and worked in close collaboration with the other Construction Management firms for several years through the start-up of the project.

As the various project teams and trades came together, we noticed what we felt were misalignments in the organizational structure, including how the job was being staffed and the way it was run. I met with the airline's top-level management to discuss what the culture of this world-class project could be. They asked me what I meant.

I said, "Well, you know, you should have a culture. You have a premier project here—you're building a whole new head-house terminal and concourses in an existing airport without shutting it down. It's a feat that's never really been done before."

The airline executive felt that the Construction Management team should dictate the process, but I asked if I could initiate the conversation, and the executive said OK. So I sat down with leadership from the Construction Management team to discuss the atmosphere that was forming on the project.

I took three or four pages of notes on where I saw gaps in organization or approaches that might snowball down the line, having seen them do it before. My goal was to identify practices that could negatively impact collaboration and problem-solving. There were a couple of main issues I emphasized:

First, there were seventeen directors on the project. There was really no need for more than three, but most importantly, by having so many "head chefs," there would be no accountability in who to answer to or for.

Second, there needed to be more team structure and organization, especially to establish that accountability. There were also some controls we could use better within the structure of the people and the philosophy to help us get there.

Thirdly, in the absence of a broader team culture, there were many mini-cultures that emerged in the gap--largely ones that existed from past projects. Anyone that wasn't a part of those previous teams wasn't in their circle of trust. You were out!

I took these findings back to the airline and shared what I thought the organization should look like, including the behavior changes

I knew we could expect by implementing the new structure. That conversation allowed our process to take shape on the project and marked the beginning of the culture shift we needed.

Over the next six months, those seventeen director-level jobs were consolidated into three main focus, or expertise, areas: one for landside, one for airside, and one for the roadways program. By having one point-person accountable for each primary segment of the project, the streamlined structure enabled the team to function more efficiently. Those directors all had the support of the people that worked for them. Each person knew precisely to whom they reported and who was responsible for what work.

It wasn't until a few years later that I was having a conversation with the airline executive about the weight of this shift. We had been invited to speak on a panel, and I asked the client to collaborate on the presentation. The client agreed, and we began discussing what the presentation should cover.

"Let's talk about how you helped reorganize and change the culture of our project."

I said, "Well, I never knew that's what happened."

The response was, "No, Mike, you did it."

I never knew that they recognized what I'd done, because it was just the right move for the project's success, and I couldn't have done it alone. Every member of the management team worked together to make it happen. There were a lot of egos involved, and it was critical that they were put away for the benefit of the project. Company hats were replaced with strategic direction and top-down support.

By enacting a culture shift in the way we did -- with the One Team. Shared Success framework we knew was successful -- the team became a TEAM in those six months. The dynamics had completely changed, because people began to work together and trust each other, which had tremendous benefits for the airline.

Several years into the project, COVID-19 created a perfect storm that significantly reduced plane and people traffic.

I said, "Listen, there's no better time to build an airport than when there are no people and no planes." The airline agreed to let us accelerate progress, having seen how efficiently we were working together. Accelerating the timeline would have been a disaster for a dysfunctional project team. But we had remained focused on the jobsite culture and philosophy amongst the team—getting them to do what needed to be done with the client's best interest in mind. The benefits of the project were huge! We finished most of the work about a year earlier than planned.

It wasn't about the design; it was about the people. Getting the people aligned and organized with the right tools in place to measure resulted in a great team.

We later brought that same team back together at another nearby airport for a new project with the airline, and the same thing continued there, with great reinforcement and dedication.

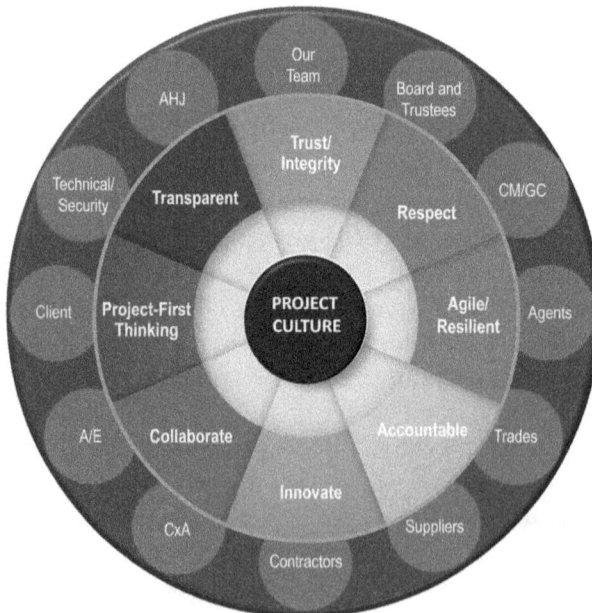

# CHAPTER 7

# CM Neutral and the Evolution of One Team. Shared Success.ˢᵐ

In the 1950s and 60s, everything was done on a general contracting basis—a lump sum price to perform contracted work. The role of the construction manager (CM) emerged as a way to get the general contractor on the side of the owner by serving as the owner's advocate.

The CM position was designed to protect the owner's best interest as trade contractors were hired to perform the work. It fell apart almost immediately because CMs had pre-existing trade relationships that created bias going into any new partnership with an owner. They could not protect all the owners' interests, because of those relationships, and oftentimes, friendships.

This dynamic was largely what I experienced in the early days of my career. As a project manager (PM), I found I could influence those relationships to everybody's advantage.

The CM Neutral method—which first materialized on that Texas highway project in the early 1990s—began with incremental interventions:

- If there was a change order in negotiations, the PM would sit with the trade (representing the owner's interests) and the CM or general contractor (GC) and negotiate those change orders.
- Once negotiations were completed, the trade contractor was paid immediately, rather than allowing for accounting's typical lag time.

- The CM's or GC's estimating team was removed and replaced by the PM's estimators.

By implementing these changes, we saved money, sped up delivery setup time, and made a lot of people happy because projects were running more smoothly. This was the genesis of the CM Neutral framework.

The shift in process was especially effective at mitigating the pressures of bending to those pre-existing relationships. The CM and the trades have to work together most directly on a project, and that sometimes means compromising the relationship between the owner and the CM, vendors, and others, for the sake of avoiding confrontation. The trades would say, "You owe me from the last job," and the CMs would bend. Over the years, many CMs said implementing our methodology helped to avoid a lot of ill will and frustration that they experienced.

We started using CM Neutral every day in the early 2000s and saved $80 million in negotiations on one of our first projects with the new system, field testing its strengths and weaknesses to identify where it could be better. We got involved with every trade negotiation. We built the schedule for the project, not for the owner's best interest or for the contractor's best interest, but for the project's best interest, and we oversaw its implementation. Our goal was a truly neutral CM position, one that could put everybody else wherever they could benefit the project most.

## Our Vision Develops

Some years later, the term "PMX" came about because the Construction Management Association (CMA) needed a term to better define program management. It was initially chosen as a broad term to cover the management of multiple projects.

By the CMA's definition, program management could mean two projects (PM squared), three projects (PM cubed), and so on. It encompassed cost control, quality control, and schedule control—all the things that generate success. If you had three or four projects running together for the same client, you could look at every light bulb and every paint color. Many things could be uniformly used across several concurrent projects to save money, decrease delivery time, or create uniformity. The X meant "exponential project management."

I disagreed with this proposal -- and actually wrote an article in *Construction News* on the subject -- because no matter how similar or connected projects are, they're still separate entities. Even when related to other parts of a multiphase program, each project has an individual flavor—needs, schedules, problems, advantages, you name it. We also are not always managing multi-project programs. Could PMX apply usefully to a single project? If so, what should the X mean?

At first, X meant the factor for complications surrounding multiple projects. As a company, we started talking about "excellence" in terms of "extraordinary, exceptional, exemplary," and other similar expressions (pun intended). It was a demand for increased quality, shared resources, and collaboration that forced us to up our game thirty years ago and became integral to our process.

Ultimately, we defined PMX as "project management to the X power." The CM Neutral idea evolved into One Team. Shared Success.[sm] as we sharpened the focus on the organization of the entire team, everyone, every company, across the entire process. "We can help make your team extraordinary, exceptional, and so on."

We do things that promote a better project by getting people to cooperate more closely. Stress in any project (in construction or other industries) is a major obstruction that leads to subpar results. When team members trust that everybody has their back—that someone probably has a solution to whatever problem might arise and is willing to share it—anxiety and ego become a nonissue. The focus stays on the project and its delivery.

## Our Goal

### Origin

The original goal of the CM Neutral method involved collaboration, avoiding project delays, and removing conflict, and that remains the intent. As we addressed its limitations and systematized its structure in the early 2000s, most deliberately and comprehensively on the Global Financial Institution's headquarters project, carefully organizing the management team to maximize the method's effectiveness is what took it to the next level—what turned it into One Team. Shared Success.℠.

Having the authority to reorganize the Institution's team—putting the right people in the right places to prioritize delivery—and studying the difference in the outcome allowed me to prove that CM Neutral worked as an intervention, but its ideas would have the greatest impact with that organizational component at the foundation. This new system, One Team. Shared Success.℠, saved years off the schedule and millions of dollars on that project.

On any construction project, but especially on the Global Financial Institution's, there are really three main areas of concern:

- **Quality control**. Is the project being built according to the design intent? Is everything straight, plumb, and level?
- **Commercial viability**. When you think you have to make a change to the project, is it an entitlement? How do you negotiate the change? Can you make this change and remain profitable?
- **Delivery**. Are we giving the clients what they're paying for? Can you bring that project to completion despite the weather, politics, changes, or anything else that's in or out of your control? How do you accomplish your tasks better or faster to achieve the project goals?

Efficient, effective organization really changes the mindset of everybody involved. Segmenting these three areas of focus into three dedicated weekly meetings streamlines the flow of decisions and actions related to each. Let's say that a commercial issue arises, and someone brings it up in the delivery meeting—the contractor says, "I have a change order outstanding. Until you pay me to make that change, I'm not doing anything."

The response should be, "Okay, but we're here to discuss delivery. That's an issue for the commercial meeting. Please bring it up there, and we'll discuss it there."

Everyone came into that room to focus on delivery, and the PM needs to insist that they stay focused on delivery. We organize the intent and the rules of every meeting, and we stick to them; that's how we stay on track. Your agenda is as critical as your schedule; it ensures that people come in with the right frame of mind and stay framed.

## Execution

The goal of this book is to prove that everyone, even the most stubborn amongst us, are capable of embracing One Team. Shared Success.<sup>sm</sup>. The key is maintaining the neutrality that CM Neutral first introduced while setting up the organization.

Owners have tried – and failed – to institute this system with a contractor alone. When we come in as a neutral third party, we tell everybody, "We're not here for the owner. We have been hired by the owner, and we're being paid by the owner, but we're here to make the best decisions for the project, based on our experience in this industry." This is what is expected of any consultant and most everyone understands that, so the proposition is easier to buy into.

When an owner does it, a certain level of distrust is expected. Even when *we* do it, there can be a certain level of distrust, but we neutralize that distrust as we perform. When we joined previous project teams, most didn't believe us straight away.

When we removed people who were obstructing the Global Financial Institution's headquarters project, *they* began to believe us. When we showed that we could save the Texas highway project a truckload of money by doing something in a new way, *they* began to believe us.

We had to prove we cared about the project above all else. We had to prove that we wanted the job to be done well for everybody concerned. The owner has a harder time convincing everyone, because the contractors think the owner is protecting their own best interest—and of course, they are.

When you can see the bigger picture, the initial resistance is a little ironic, because the whole point of the One Team. Shared Success. ˢᵐ approach is that if it's in *the contractors' best interest* then, in the long run, it's also in *the owner's best interest* and vice versa.

I tell the owner from the beginning, "We're not your hired gun. We're here as a neutral party. If you have a change order that you owe, we're going to tell you that. We want everybody to be happy, so we're not taking sides, *ever!*" My experience also tells me that it's important to get people to discuss things honestly and open up about how things are actually going, and then collaborate on solutions to the problems. This allows people to trust the work environment and change the way they operate.

If an owner remains neutral, collaborative, and solutions-driven consistently, they can pull it off, but it takes time to change behavior at scale. It took six months in one of the stories I shared, a year in another, to see the process working. Most owners tend to get frustrated when it doesn't happen right away, which shouldn't surprise anyone; it's their money being spent, and they don't want to overspend on a project any more than you want to overspend at the grocery store or gas station.

Maybe you're not an owner or a CEO, but you answer to one -- to some degree, you have "third party power." Use it to your advantage to establish trust and get people working together.

No matter where you sit, when you have a contract, you must collaborate. You have to be part of the resolution of problems, not the cause. You can't be the person who says, "You owe me this, you owe me that, it's your fault, not mine, so go fix it." Many times, I've heard owners say, "That's not their job to do that." This attitude creates the kind of work environment I encountered at the Ivy League Institution -- one where people are not actively helping one another, because it's not "their job" to do so. An owner can and should reasonably expect people to perform the jobs they're hired and being paid for; again, it's their money being spent. Tightly controlling those job descriptions, however, shifts the focus to what is or isn't in scope, rather than how the project can best be completed.

The same goes for the owners, themselves. They are experts in their fields. If they don't open up that expertise to anybody on the management team who might need advice, that owner's cheating them out of a valuable resource. They are now the obstacle to success.

Teamwork cannot be overemphasized—collaboration is vital to success.

It should be obvious, but to many, it still isn't. Everybody in that room has a stake in the successful resolution of every problem. Logic dictates that everybody should help solve problems if they can, because every problem is a potential delay or rework, and that's where people lose money. Once you start to eat up time or redo things, your potential profit decreases.

Take quick action, resolve the problem, and forget (for the moment) who caused the problem. Get it out of the way and move on. That's the best practice, not just in construction, but also everywhere!

Sometimes, an owner can do that by themselves; at other times, the owner can't. In those instances, a third party must come in and be a mitigator or mediator. It's not always necessary for the entire duration of the project if the team is retrained properly and completely. It takes time, which owners often do not feel they have, and patience to change how the team is aligned, their behaviors, and the project culture. Once those changes begin to feel habitual, they should become an instinctual part of meetings and the workplace.

The pitfalls are many, and it's important to be aware of them, but they can be overcome. If you're doing this on your own—and when I do this among people who don't know me, I'm somewhat on my own—you must go in, plant the seed for teamwork, and nurture its growth.

How do you do that? What's the very first thing?

- **Be honest** with everybody about what you're doing and what you hope to accomplish by doing it. That sets the stage and gives everybody an identical set of expectations.
- **Be open** with them as you want them to be with you.
- **Be consistent**. Set the rules and follow them all the way—every week and every day, among every subcontractor and tradesman. Set an example—practice what you preach.
- **Be blunt**. When you see a problem, say, "Here's what I see as the problem, and here's what I see as the fix," or "Here's what I see as the problem. What possible fixes can you give me?"

I think "radical honesty," "radical dependability," "radical transparency," and "radical candor" are not too strong a set of phrases for what I'm outlining. Just like in those old Hollywood Westerns, being a straight shooter gets you a reputation.

It should go without saying, but I'll say it anyway: Every single person on your team has to come to the table with the same honesty, openness, candor, and "can-do" willingness to get it done right. It will take time for the habit to develop, but when you lay out the plan, ask them straight up, "I know this is new, but are you willing to give it a chance? Are you willing to try a different approach?"

If someone is not willing to try, it might be time to look for somebody else in that role.

Your goal, by implementing these strategies, is to get people to rally around the ideas. Construction is, traditionally, a very masculine career path, and today's jobsite differs only a little from what it was a century ago. Today, it's tough men and tough women, drinking beer, swearing a blue streak, and doing hard, physical labor in all kinds of weather. But at the end of the day, they're just people. They go to work to feed their families, and they worry about their future as much as you or me.

When you get it down to the personal level, they appreciate the help, and they'll buy into new ideas as they see them working. They don't want to work harder than necessary. They don't want to lose work days due to delays. They want their worksite to be as safe a place as possible. They want to go home in one piece at the end of shift. Like any normal person, they appreciate it when they see someone walking the jobsite helping them do a better job.

In the next three chapters, I will walk you through the three corner-stones of One Team. Shared Success.sm: alignment, organization, and tools and analytics.

# CHAPTER 8

# The Evolution of One Team. Shared Success.<sup>sm</sup> The First Step: Alignment

## Our Operating Philosophy

### Environment

When things go well, you don't need a consultant. Consultants are designed to bring a new, and perhaps, different perspective or experience that the current employees don't have. Sometimes it takes an outsider's view to suggest a new way of working, a new corporate culture.

In my experience, the culture of a project team is the bedrock of its success. It encompasses shared values, norms, and practices that not only shape our interactions but also influence how we communicate, collaborate, solve problems, and make decisions. A positive team culture is one that fosters trust, encourages open communication, promotes accountability, and supports innovation. When team members feel valued and motivated, they are more likely to contribute effectively towards achieving project goals. This supportive environment is essential for enhancing productivity, meeting deadlines, and ensuring the overall success of the project. Throughout my career, I've seen firsthand how cultivating such a culture can lead to remarkable outcomes, transforming the way teams operate and delivering success beyond expectations. I've said it before, and I'll say it again: If one person fails, we all fail. It all comes down to how we treat one another.

If these kinds of cultures were the norm, we wouldn't need consultants. The reality is that people struggle to play well with others.

There are a hundred reasons why this happens; it could be fear, anxiety, ego, lack of technical skills, or lack of people skills. These are your problems, and any one of them can make a person difficult to work with -- that's your symptom.

In the early days of my career, I would let a bad working environment dictate my behavior. I was very likely to end up being a jackass, unhappy, and unproductive, and probably did not treat others the way I should have. I didn't care about the team or the project; I was just focused on a buck and getting out of there. I didn't know any better. Dealing with people on this level is kind of like hacking at twigs on a tree—a lot of work for small returns.

When you deal with any team, you deal with their anxieties and fears and offended feelings toward each other, as well as their positive aspects. Lack of alignment—team members that can't get along—are symptoms of something going on much deeper in the roots of the organization. My behavior was just that - a sign that the working environment was not a positive one. Your boss can say to you, "Well, look, Smith, or look, Jones, you need to be a team player," and I am sure you'll do your best, but if the root of the problem is a toxic work environment, if the company doesn't recognize and deal with the cause, no one will be working at their peak.

When I joined the Global Financial Institution's headquarters project, I was given the authority as PM to remove people who interfered with the mission in order to create a culture of collaboration—those who were not Project-First Thinkers. The Institution's ADF wouldn't talk to the contractor's COO. They hated each other; they wouldn't even be in the same room together. That wasn't the actual problem, though it certainly wasn't helping. Their lack of cooperation set a tone and a precedent, so others acted the same way. *That* was a problem, and they had to be removed.

Those who remained said, "This one is serious. This one is removing problems." I had proven to them that I was always going to put the project first, and we worked together to create a new culture of cooperation, which made them stronger in their jobs because they knew their teammates were working with them, not against them.

Did I just tell the ADF and the PEx, "You're a problem, you're out"?

Did I warn them and give them a chance to reform, with something like, "Look, what you're doing is causing problems with the team. I don't want to remove you, but we need to fix this"?

Did I give them a proverbial "shot across the bow"?

I had to show the team that I was serious. Sometimes, you need a general practitioner who'll bandage your wounds and help you heal. At other times, you need a surgeon who'll rush you into the operating room to amputate a gangrenous limb.

In this case, these two had gangrene, these two were **culture killers**; they had to be removed.

## Project-First Thinking

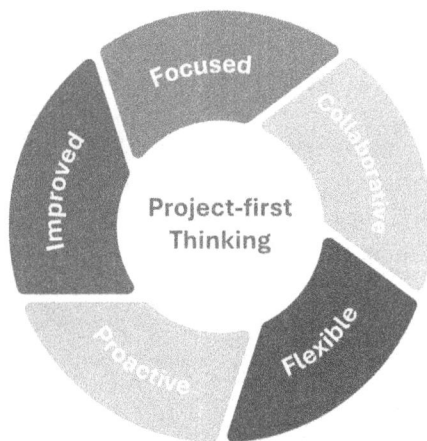

Project-First Thinking is a proactive and strategic mindset that prioritizes the success of the project above individual or company preferences or interests. Focusing on the project's needs during decision-making processes and proactively addressing challenges enhances the project team's likelihood of achieving successful outcomes. There are a few key aspects:

- **Focus on the project's goals**. This approach emphasizes aligning all efforts and decisions with the overarching goals and objectives of the project. It ensures that every action taken contributes to moving the project forward and achieving its desired outcomes.
- **Collaborative decision-making**. Project-First Thinking encourages collaboration among team members, stakeholders, and partners to ensure that decisions are made with the project's best interests in mind. This includes actively seeking input from all relevant parties and considering various perspectives before making decisions. It requires trust.
- **Flexibility and adaptability**. Projects often encounter unexpected challenges and changes. Project-First Thinking necessitates being flexible and adaptable in response to these challenges, while maintaining the focus on finding solutions that keep the project on track and aligned with its goals.
- **Risk management**. Understanding and managing risks is crucial for project success. Project-First Thinking involves identifying potential risks early on, assessing their potential impact on the project, and proactively implementing strategies to mitigate them.
- **Continuous improvement**. Project-First Thinking emphasizes the importance of continuously evaluating and improving processes and outcomes. This includes seeking feedback, analyzing performance metrics, making adjustments as needed to enhance project effectiveness and efficiency, and crucially, fostering relationships with respect while seeking to mentor or provide support to team members.

By adopting a project-first approach, teams stay focused on the outcome and increase their chances of delivering a successful one.

This mindset is also important for reinforcing neutrality across the team. It doesn't matter what your title is or what company is on your hard hat. At the end of the day, the work you do with and for your employer's clients generates revenue for your employer. That revenue ensures your paycheck won't bounce.

You want people to say, "I am employed by ZZZ, Inc., but I'm working for *this project*. I'm dedicating my resources–training, experience, intelligence, physical strength, my heart and soul–to delivering this project. I'm going to think outside that box, be innovative, be disruptive of the status quo, and do what it takes because that strengthens my company's reputation." That's the long view. Whatever task you undertake each day, do it to the best of your ability. That's the short view that makes the long view possible.

Remember the Chinese proverb, "The journey of a thousand miles begins with a single step"? Every project represents a few steps along the journey to your company's long-term profitability and your job security.

You'd better not trip over a stone, or worse, your own feet.

This is Project-First Thinking. It's what gets everybody aligned on that all-important first step in making a project work. This approach eliminates the fear of being a little bold sometimes: Fear that you cannot speak up and share ideas because you'll be criticized. Fear of just being there for your team and it being perceived as "interfering." Fear that they don't need your expertise and so, you're not important. Remove those fears, and you're on the road to making *this project* shine.

Be honest upfront. Don't be afraid to tell the hard truths; it hurts less that way.

When I was brutally honest, I found that it encouraged people to start talking to each other. They utilized individual strengths to cover others' individual weaknesses, and they made it work. That's the whole alignment and team thing in a nutshell–getting people together and *creating synergy*.

When executed correctly, positive transformations occur. Conflicts diminish, team members collaborate effectively and seek support when necessary. Blame gives way to proactive problem-solving. The project operates more smoothly, and a more cohesive and focused team emerges. These experiences on projects throughout my career taught me that you can take a very negative situation—in some cases, an impossible situation—and turn it into a very positive one. That's what I've been trying to do ever since.

I've heard the CM and Trades say:

> *In past projects, we've started getting to this level, and people started seeing improvement. But we never experienced all the way to this level. The owners of the CM and Trades came by and said, "Hey, we are making money all of a sudden. What's going on there?" Their productivity has gone way up. They're happier working on this project. The team is all aligned. Things started to change, even for the company principals. It's like caveman to man, an evolutionary process. It takes time, but once we get there, we don't want to go back.*

These kinds of endorsements of the process—of the way One Team. Shared Success.[sm] disrupts the status quo for everyone for the better—are rewarding. People *see* the change. But in business, everything has a number - even culture. In 2015, the Culture Think Tank developed a method for measuring the four states of culture (distracting, neutral, contributing, and performing) and assigning KPI's. This scoring system allows projects and organizations to directly determine the strength of their culture at any point in time and make adjustments for corrective action.[11]

By creating alignment on the Global Financial Institution's headquarters project, we saw our own performance metrics improve on average by about 30 percent; that's significant improvement and everyone will notice.

---

[11] The Culture Think Tank. (2024). The Culture Assessment. https://www.the-culturethinktank.com/culture-assessment/

**Making the Shift to a World-class Project Team**

Project teams can vary widely in their performance and attitude, ranging from combative to world-class. Each type of team presents unique challenges and outcomes based on their approach to work and interaction with each other.

1. **Combative**. These teams are characterized by minimal work completion and a hostile environment. The focus often shifts from project goals to preparing for litigation, as conflicts escalate into an "us versus them" mentality. Productivity is severely hampered by distrust and continuous friction among team members. I would describe the team I joined initially at the Global Financial Institution as combative.

2. **Business as usual**. Teams operating under this banner maintain a peaceful coexistence primarily through conflict avoidance. They tend to assign blame based on circumstances rather than addressing underlying issues. While they meet client expectations minimally, the lack of proactive engagement and innovation prevents any notable success or improvement. The Ivy League Institution's team was roughly functioning this way.

3. **Good**. These teams meet essential project criteria, such as schedule, budget, and quality standards. Traditional teamwork is evident, and while the client is satisfied, the process to get there is often painful. However, these teams manage to avoid litigation, indicating a basic level of functional cooperation and problem-solving.

4. **World-class.** At the pinnacle of performance are world-class teams, where members are highly motivated, empowered, and supportive of one another. These teams excel in resolving conflicts efficiently and fostering an environment where excuses are unnecessary. By creating a robust framework for addressing challenges, the team remains harmonious and productive. Their collaborative spirit and proactive approach keep the client satisfied and confident in the team's ability to deliver outstanding results. High-performance culture not only meets but often exceeds client expectations, resulting in exceptional satisfaction and success.

From combative to world-class, the evolution of project teams is marked by significant changes in collaboration, problem-solving, and overall attitude towards work and each other. Each level represents a step towards more sophisticated and effective project management and execution.

Is a world-class team too good to be true? I've built and seen them in action, so I know with certainty that it's not. The stories I've shared and the framework those experiences helped me to create are evidence that team transformation is not just possible, it's formulaic. Aligning the team, shifting the mindset to Project-First thinking, removing obstacles -- this is *how*.

I can't say it enough: these are the things that must be done to develop a team that not only meets expectations, but consistently exceeds them, setting new standards for excellence in project delivery. Here is what else you can expect when you change the team's behavior from combative to world-class:

- Not limited by contractual requirements.
- Passion, extraordinary personal commitment, intrinsic satisfaction, and pride.
- Organizational lines are blurred, and team members do "whatever it takes" to get the job done.
- Team owns the game regardless of the circumstances, no excuses—fully empowered at all levels.
- Conflicts strengthen the team and create opportunities for breakthroughs.
- Outside-of-the-box thinking by the entire partnership. Open to new technologies and processes.
- Open, direct verbal communication that is sometimes confrontational but never personal and always constructive.
- Client's delighted.
- Lifelong relationships cultivate future opportunities.
- Trusted business advisor.

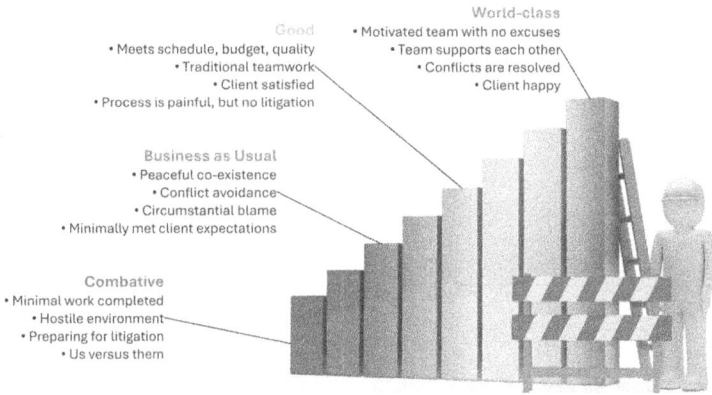

**World-class**
- Motivated team with no excuses
- Team supports each other
- Conflicts are resolved
- Client happy

**Good**
- Meets schedule, budget, quality
- Traditional teamwork
- Client satisfied
- Process is painful, but no litigation

**Business as Usual**
- Peaceful co-existence
- Conflict avoidance
- Circumstantial blame
- Minimally met client expectations

**Combative**
- Minimal work completed
- Hostile environment
- Preparing for litigation
- Us versus them

From combative to world-class team

# CHAPTER 9

# The Evolution of One Team. Shared Success.[sm] The Second Step: Organization – Delivery, Commercial, QA/QC

## Delivery Is Paramount

CM Neutral began with this straightforward idea: "Make things simpler. Share resources and collaborate."

Delivery is central to the organization.

That meant streamlining the meeting schedule – one for quality control, one for commercial viability, one for delivery. The goal of the delivery meeting is to discuss only the actual work issues. When meetings lack structure or an agenda or a clear leader, it's easy to get bogged down by other issues, slowing progress to a crawl. One Team. Shared Success.[sm] organizes a time and place for all these discussions to keep all of the agendas moving forward.

## The Delivery Team

The team's alignment around Project-First Thinking is an important factor in the success of the reorganized meeting schedule; this is one of the reasons why alignment is the first cornerstone of One Team. Shared Success.ˢᵐ. It has to be in place for the system to function effectively. A good team goes into the delivery meeting thinking, "When we get out of that meeting, we're done. We've resolved it, and we're moving on. How do we all resolve this problem without letting it go beyond this meeting?" No one walks in ready to point fingers or lay blame for a particular problem; the focus of the conversation is on coming up with the best solutions—the ones with minimal impact on the scheduling or cost. In fact, most of the time, when the discussion was structured this way, there was no cost or schedule impact. If a trade contractor is making money, the owner is saving money.

At this point, you may be thinking, "Wait, you wrote earlier that someone asked permission to 'yell' at another team member, and you gave it because they deserved to be 'yelled' at." There's an important distinction to be made here between blame and course correction, and what you as a leader can allow to take place in the delivery meeting. The goal wasn't to reprimand or embarrass anyone; we paused for a minute, and it was over. Everyone laughed, and we were back to solving problems. Let me be clear: When mistakes are made, a remedy is necessary, and disciplinary action can be applied. That discipline might be termination if the mistake is that serious. That's rare; usually, a simple explanation, some additional training, and applying a fix that's already available is enough, and we move on. You have to call out the patterns to prevent them in the future.

Disciplinary action, however, is not the function of the delivery meeting. That needs to come later, and it must take place in private. It must be done respectfully and politely. It must be done on the assumption that it was a mistake—don't act like it was a conspiracy to bring down civilization as we know it. Few among us are anywhere near that ambitious. Remember: When you deal with any team, you deal with their fears, anxieties, egos, and skills, or lack thereof. Mistakes are symptoms of these problems, and you cannot treat the symptom without treating the root problem – at least not effectively.

**Delivery**

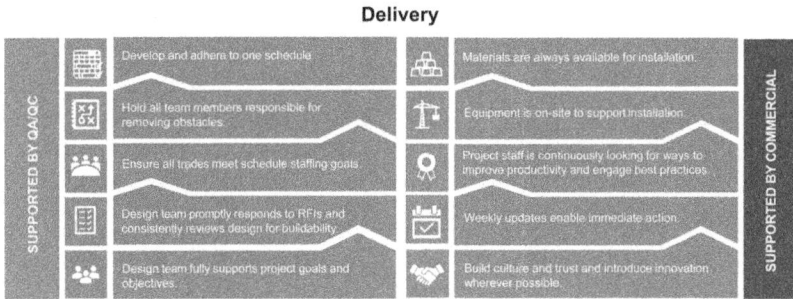

What we call the Golden Rule has had a place in every philosophy and culture. "Do unto others as you would have them do unto you" is good advice, so take it. That attitude adds to the positive work environment. Punitive retribution—punishment for the sake of punishment or negative reinforcement, as it's sometimes called—causes fear. Fear leads people to hide problems, which makes it harder to find solutions.

### Shhh, It Happens.

Obstacles to the delivery are unavoidable:

- Sometimes, as we've discussed, a person's skill or experience isn't at the level where they need to be.
- Sometimes, a situation arises, and the people involved don't choose the best way to deal with it.
- Sometimes, storms, fires, floods, plagues, and other "acts of God" present themselves, and we just have to get out of the way until it blows over.

These all can cause delays; delays cost money and can ruin a good work environment. The One Team. Shared Success.[sm] system puts practices in place to deal with those potential problems:

- Organize the management team—align them and keep them aligned.
- Schedule meetings—delivery, commercial, QA/QC—and don't cancel or postpone them. Set and follow an agenda for each meeting.

- Get delivery right; establish clearly defined goals and objectives at the beginning, then work toward them.
- Acquire the tools and analytics to measure the product, the goals, and the objectives. Make sure that people meet those KPIs.

This is the framework I stress-tested when working for the Global Financial Institution. Given it was my first experience on such an immense project with immense problems, I needed proof--both for myself and anyone else--that it worked. Our KPIs suggested that team alignment brought about a 30 percent improvement in production, team commitment, and task completion. The organization was responsible for 50 percent, and tools and analytics 20 percent. The organization clearly made the biggest impact; taking command of and optimizing this piece is what evolved One Team. Shared Success.[sm]. Alignment is the driving force behind that organization, with tools and analytics keeping things moving in the right direction.

The delivery-focused organization was the game changer. Within the first month, I saw attitudes begin to change as I saw language change. It wasn't just the end of the swearing at each other, either, although that was a definite sign of a more positive environment! You cannot imagine my joy the first time I heard someone start to talk about change orders in a meeting and the other person responded, "We're here to talk about delivery. Save that for commercial."

That single sentence changed the team dynamic. It wasn't the "outsider" (whether me or any other consultant) telling them—it was one of their own. When one or two of them bought into the "rules" of the process, that allowed the others to really buy into it without hesitation. This is important in any business where you are exercising these strategies; if you are coming in externally, you need to have allies that will help model the behavior. The same is true if you're operating internally.

Let's face it, even if you know it's a good idea, most of us really don't want to be the first to say so. We don't want to risk ridicule if the others haven't come to the same conclusion. It's human nature to let somebody else go first. Once that happened, the mission and goals fell into place.

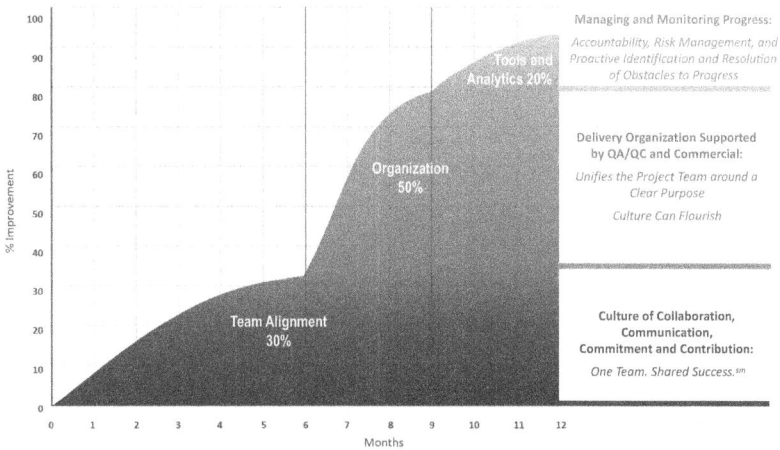

Impact on Project Team Performance

## One Team. Shared Success.ˢᵐ

At 20 percent, tools and analytics have a somewhat smaller, but still significant role to play in improving team culture and effectiveness. In a project-first or delivery-first mindset, any area that can be optimized should be.

When a report would indicate that things didn't go as well as we had hoped during the previous week, they asked, "How do we improve this week?" Everyone was being measured in a way that was new to them, and the data turned out to be a tool that encouraged everybody to up their game. When we said to ourselves, "Great job last week," it meant that each team member saw what they did and how they positively impacted the project. But "they" never meant some of them; "they" always meant all of them.

That's the recipe for success, as it was for the Global Financial Institution.

Most of you who are reading this have probably heard the old expression "Paying for the big marbles, but not the rest." It's an analogy. Imagine that you've filled a jar with big marbles. This is the work you're giving to your staff–your management team–to accomplish. Is the jar full? No, you can still fit smaller marbles in between and among the larger. Then, among the smaller marbles, you can fit tiny marbles. And smaller, and smaller, and so on, forever–theoretically. Those small marbles are the mini projects that make up the big project. The tiny marbles are care and attention, individual responsibility for doing the job right. They're also consideration for the client–the idea that you won't waste the client's time and money by doing substandard work.

Those tiny marbles can be difficult to quantify. It can be a challenge to find people who can play with them. It can be very easy to lose them. Treat them carefully.

## Rewards

The obvious and simplest reward is money.

"We've scheduled A amount of work that will require B days. If you complete A amount of work C days earlier, you get $D extra." I doubt you'll ever meet anyone who will object to such a plan.

Also, a bigger paycheck is tangible. It has the immediate (but temporary) effect of making someone's life better, and it's easy to calculate, track, and analyze.

But that's only one way to approach financial rewards.

On one project, I met with several of the trade subcontractors to talk about what we're trying to accomplish, and I learned just how far simple appreciation can get you. By "appreciation," I mean just telling them they did a good job. Imagine, every week, the PM or CM comes into the delivery meeting and says, "Hey, we started every activity this week on the early start date. Awesome work, folks!"

Our CPM schedule had early and late start and finish dates clearly spelled out for each activity. If you go past the late finish date, then other people get delayed. If enough activities aren't completed until after the late finish date, the entire project goes critical. Delays like this were commonplace enough in my experience in the 1990s, that I wondered: "Why are we not always starting on the early dates?" If all the prior activities have been completed, why not go forward? Surprisingly, many didn't, so I started tracking those dates.

People asked, "Why are you doing that?"

I answered, "Because, if you start early, you finish early. If you finish early, the chance of delaying tasks that follow is minimized." When I started putting that philosophy out to contractors, they resisted initially.

Pretty quickly thereafter, we could walk into our meetings and say, "By the way, ninety-five percent of activities were initiated on their early start dates." They began to see the benefit, particularly for planning resources more effectively and efficiently. The schedule laid out the resources that each group knew they'd need to do a particular activity. When a project operates in late-start mode, those resources stack up on top of each other. They take up space on the jobsite that could better be used for other things. Late finishes may force you to work on top of an electrician or a carpenter because you're not out of their way on time.

When all the other trades are working the schedule properly, no one is underfoot of others, and no one is in a critical mess anymore. The simple solution, in this case, was, "We're starting early because we can and want to."

Why did they want to? It wasn't just the money; it was also about reputation. Imagine going to bid on a job and being able to say in the pitch, "We completed every activity on our last three [or six or ten] contracts on or before the early finish date." That kind of track record should get the attention of whoever is making hiring decisions.

The most well-received appreciation can be simple, too—people like being told, "You did well." When the project isn't in critical condition, you have some flexibility to host a lunch or a dinner for an outstanding crew. That's a good place to stand up and say, "You're doing a great job. Look what you did. You were told that it was impossible, but you did it anyway."

That's exactly what happened at the Global Financial Institution. I was reviewing the schedule one day with the director of transition and customer success, who was overseeing one piece of the project, and we were discussing the amount of time needed before the Institution's staff could move into the completed floors after the temporary certificate of occupancy was issued. I said to that director, "You have twenty-six weeks scheduled for this task, but I'm giving you six."

"How can you give me six?"

"That's all you need."

"Mike, this has been taking me twenty-six weeks." The director was right, but so was I. I had stopped the bleeding and was ripping off all the Band-Aids that were put in place over the years, and it hurt, at least initially.

"Because you've had every obstacle in your way. I'm taking all the obstacles out of the way." The director's boss, the chief executive of the institution, backed me up, "Whatever Mike says is what you've got to do."

After we made those scheduled completion dates—twice!—he said, "Mike, this is great. It's the most successful we've ever been." Of course, it was. Imagine going from needing half a year to complete a task to completing that task in just over a month; they were working at nearly six times their former pace. They were all challenged in a way that made them do the best they could do. They did it—and an amazing job they did—and if they bragged about it, they deserved to.

They had to be pushed, but they had to be the ones that decided to go for it. That team worked together, and they benefited. For the first time in four years, that contractor was making money. Nothing had changed about the price of the work; they made money because they were more productive.

One final reward -- one of those tiny, very intangible, but potentially vital, marbles -- is the building of long-lasting relationships. We're co-workers, that's what we get paid for, but if we're a fully aligned team, we're also friends -- not out of obligation, but because of trust. That connection should last long beyond the end of the project. I have relationships with many former co-workers from projects decades ago, and we enjoy keeping in touch.

At the end of the workday, life isn't over, and no one has too many friends.

When you bid on future projects, your reputation will get you more work than low-balling or having to twist someone's arm.

## A Side Note

Of course, rewards that are tangible tend to be the most exciting, but they don't have to be project or campaign-specific. As leaders, we must motivate our people not just during a sprint, but also over the sustained long-term.

As I wrote this book, I was experimenting with different reward systems within our own organization through the lens of succession planning -- which I see as an opportunity to get a ten-thousand-foot view of the situation. It's a chance to reach down into the organization and say things like "You know, you've been successful on multiple projects, and we're thinking about your role in leadership down the line. As an immediate reward for the good work you've done, we're giving you a car allowance."

We also discussed other incentives, like basketball tickets, monetary bonuses, and tuition assistance. The goal is to motivate people to strive to do better by recognizing what they've already done.

Remember: it's a reward – not a carrot. The people that receive them are those who have performed the best. There are as many ways to reward people as there are people, and it's important that you do it.

Growing up, I never heard, "Mike, here's an extra thousand dollars." I definitely never got courtside seats. I earned a measure of professional respect for doing well in what I did, but desiring rewards—verbal compliments or tangible prizes—is part of human nature. We remember when they come, and we remember when they don't.

As leaders, we have the opportunity to learn from our experiences (or grievances) and treat our people the way we would have wanted to be treated. Don't make them walk to school uphill in the snow both ways because you had to; reward them because they have worked hard, and you know you would have wanted to be rewarded, too.

## Challenges

Let me share an example:

In 1995, I was hired by an airport authority's design-build team to course-correct the construction of an automated passenger-mover system; the project was severely behind schedule, costs were ballooning, and the whole team refused to talk to each other. Sound familiar? The owner-client was on one side, the contractor/designer on the other, and the project management team sat in between. There was a lot of space, figuratively speaking, between them all. Could I get everybody talking to each other? After that first meeting, I honestly wasn't sure. Anytime anybody said anything, somebody else snapped back. It was bad.

I went back to the airport authority, and they asked, "By the way, how's the schedule shaping up?" They expected the job to be done and operational four months from the day I arrived. That was not going to happen.

I told them, "Job completion is a year and a half away, at a minimum."

That did not go over well. "What do you mean?"

"You still have steel to erect, for one. An automated train system also requires a minimum of a full year to test and commission after its built. You can't just put it into service with people's lives at stake." Safety must be tested and certified, but there were many other considerations that had to be addressed, as well. "So," I asked, "does anybody in this room want to compromise that year and possibly get sued at the end of this job because you didn't let the system mature?" Needless to say, they adopted a new schedule.

I don't know who suggested it could be done in four months or what political or economic pressure, if any, they were under, and it didn't really matter. I was responsible for fixing the problems, not pointing fingers. Priority number one was aligning that management team, and that meant being realistic and transparent about what was feasible. With the schedule reorganized and the project team on track, the cooperative was so happy with the process that they said, "We now want you to manage the automated control software system."

"I've never done that before in my life."

"It doesn't matter. Go out there, and figure this out."

Sometimes, one of the rewards for doing a great job is getting a harder job. But it's not always so bad to be a "victim" of your success.

The automated control system was being developed by a major international software company. Tech really wasn't my wheelhouse, but that challenge presented a unique opportunity to test the ideas behind One Team. Shared Success.[sm] outside of the bounds of construction – and that was exciting.

The set-up was the same. I gathered their team together and said, "Okay, this is how I want to run this job: I don't want anybody doing anything without the other people knowing, because we're all on the same team and we'll all work together."

For this job, my natural ability to get everyone in a room and aligned on the goal would not solve the real hurdle of getting the control system commissioned. That hinged on physical assets and software, which required the developer's technical expertise to deliver. One of the developers joined our management team to help bridge my technical knowledge gap so that we could execute most effectively. When the developer saw that we were getting things done in a way that was productive and meaningful, the tech wizards did what they needed to do on their end.

In the end, we delivered the automated passenger train and its control system a week early–exactly a year and a half after I told the airport authority it would take that long at minimum to accomplish. It took everything we had to get it completed and certified in that time frame, but we did it.

Be honest upfront. Don't be afraid to tell the hard truths; in the long run, it hurts less.

When I was brutally honest, they started talking to each other, they utilized one person's strengths to cover others' weaknesses, and they made it work. That's the whole idea of alignment and teamwork in a nutshell–getting people together. It's *synergy*.

This experience served as another example of the team's ability to turn a very negative situation–in this case, an impossible situation–into a very positive one.

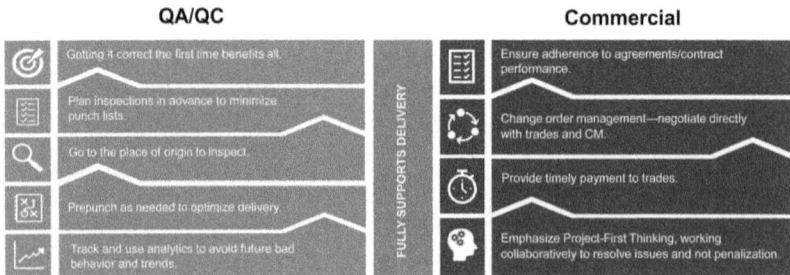

**QA/QC**

- Getting it correct the first time benefits all.
- Plan inspections in advance to minimize punch lists.
- Go to the place of origin to inspect.
- Prepunch as needed to optimize delivery.
- Track and use analytics to avoid future bad behavior and trends.

FULLY SUPPORTS DELIVERY

**Commercial**

- Ensure adherence to agreements/contract performance.
- Change order management—negotiate directly with trades and CM.
- Provide timely payment to trades.
- Emphasize Project-First Thinking, working collaboratively to resolve issues and not penalization.

## Commercial

A "commercial issue" refers to potential or real changes in the contracts, agreements, drawings, or specifications, etc.

Every member of the team has a contract. On the construction side, you've got a CM or GC, the trades, suppliers, and on the client side, the owner and the consultants. Add all those contracts up, and you have the totality of what each firm has committed to do or provide.

Contracts generally only come out where there are problems, and whoever is waiving them around is likely to be in a combative mood. "You said *this*, and now it's *that*." Sometimes it's, "I don't want it *this* way anymore, I want it like *that*." You've seen me refer to some of these commercial issues as change orders; they tend to pile up on a poorly managed project, and they can have serious legal and financial implications.

The first rule is to never go to commercial issues unless you have no other choice. Then, when you're all out of options, still do not go to commercial issues. You do not, under any circumstances, want anyone to lawyer up. One of the critical aspects of One Team. Shared Success.℠ is getting people talking. When they're talking, they can resolve things in-house, with open discussion and compromise before problems get out of hand.

On those rare occasions when the issue cannot be avoided, the meeting structure provides a place to safely discuss contractual issues. That's what you want: a serious, professional conversation defining exactly what problem has arisen and how to deal with it. When I did this in the Global Financial Institution's headquarters building, a commercial meeting was extraordinarily rare. The delivery meetings were held every week, about a hundred of them. By using them properly, we were able to limit commercial meetings to, as I recall, just two.

## The Environment

There's a lot of talk about "safe spaces" these days. Construction workers tend to speak their minds, and they often aren't afraid to use some very colorful metaphors or offend someone. Even still, many of them hesitate to speak up about certain issues, like money, because it's not unusual to get the boot when contractual issues arise. No one wants to join that exodus, so they bury them.

Those issues, however, have a way of resurfacing when they are much larger and more expensive to deal with. "Safe spaces" are key to their prevention. Management needs to create an environment where someone can come in with a commercial issue, knowing that they can say whatever's on their mind, and they won't be judged or fired for speaking out. It's more about trust, rather than safety, but both are important to establish. How does that happen?

Everything I've shared about Project-First Thinking—professionalism, accountability, collaboration, and communication—fosters a positive work environment and builds a happy team. When your people know you respect them, their work, and their opinions, they will return that respect. When you ask their opinions, they know they can share it honestly. You don't have to build a safe space if the whole work environment is safe. That foundation will enable serious, productive discussions on contractual issues -- emphasis on the productive.

Not every change is a contract issue, so it's important for everyone -- the CMs, GCs, and the client -- to go into these meetings with an open mind. Remember: the focus is the solution.

Think about it this way: On a given project, I've been to fifty or seventy-five or more than <u>one hundred</u> delivery meetings with the management group, and those meetings were very successful. I'm not going to chance to screw all that up by mishandling one commercial meeting. If I do, I'll just be tearing up work done correctly because I've done work incorrectly, and now it all has to be rebuilt.

Let's say the client says, "I want these doors moved from here to there."

The response is, "Okay, that's a contract issue. Let's talk about the contract. These doors are already built, so this change will cost money and take time. It'll put us over the budget and timetable you agreed to for this project. These changes mean this many dollars and this many days. Are you willing to absorb that cost?"

You negotiate on the details, and you eventually reach an agreement. The changes become an amendment to the contract, and everyone is satisfied they got a fair deal.

If, however, the client kicks off the discussion by yelling about how the doors were put in wrong when they were put in exactly where the architect said they should be, that's a completely different situation and one we want to avoid.

I won't engage with any client setting that tone for a conversation. Once they've calmed down, I'm happy to discuss the problem, but that kind of attitude won't be tolerated in any project meeting from anyone on the team. A very smart person once said there were two types of people in the world: people who are proactive and people who are reactive. In any conflict situation, stand your ground but don't react; be proactive, and you'll maintain control of the meeting.

To determine if the change is a contract issue, you always follow the rules of entitlement. "Entitlement" answers the question "Is this really a substantive change to?" Before you go to the commercial meeting, do your homework; perform an initial scoping or investigation. If you don't, they may respond with far more work than is really needed--which translates to more dollars, people, time in the schedule, and legal issues.

So, I tell people, "Don't escalate this immediately. Let's talk about entitlement first. Let's go to that room and see if we do have a commercial issue." I might also give it to the architect for another perspective on why - or why not - something might be entitled. This can save you a lot of time, effort, and frustration.

A simple door into a room is a smaller fix, so it's possibly not an entitlement. Redesigning the main entry for a larger vestibule might involve zoning, altering public sidewalks, amongst other considerations; that clearly is an entitlement.

If you're getting the right people together to meet every week, the smaller things can be easily resolved. I don't mind talking about entitlement in a delivery meeting, because the answer might be obvious. We may say, "Yeah, go ahead, you're right, it's a change." Once that determination has been made, we decide how to deliver that change. The commercial meeting is where we discuss how those changes affect the delivery of other aspects in the contract. The distinction is important, because one conversation allows that piece of the project to continue moving forward; the other is for the implications.

## The Entitlement and the Work

Once it's been established that there's an entitlement, the change is promptly priced and scheduled to ensure the work gets delivered in a timely fashion—meaning before it causes a delay in the next round of operations. Often when working for an owner, it's standard to negotiate with a CM or GC on a change. Over the years, I've learned it's much more effective to go directly to the trade contractors who will be executing the work. This is something that has to be written into the contract, just as it was for the Global Financial Institution, because some CMs or GCs don't want interference. Our contract rider ensures we maintain access to that direct line of communication. Everyone is invited to the meeting, but we handle the negotiation. As part of that process, once we agree on a price for the change, I guarantee payment to them within thirty days, and I make sure that it's paid. That's a critical piece of the CM Neutral philosophy. I've mentioned that it's not uncommon for change orders to take months to be processed and paid--if we're working as a team, that can't fly. We don't screw around with each other's livelihoods. The contractor should not be waiting, as some have, for six months to a year to be compensated for completed work. That's not the culture that moves us all forward together. We set the cost, the client agrees to it and processes the payment, and we move on.

## The Bottom of the Pile

In construction, projects can take anywhere from six months to ten years to complete. Inevitably, some of the many thousands of variables involved won't work out the way they were planned.

If there is not a system for dealing with commercial issues–a set procedure that everybody understands–those issues can end up at the bottom of the priority list. When they aren't addressed until the very end of the job, everybody settles for less than the best work, because there isn't time to do better, and nobody's satisfied.

I cannot repeat this point enough: resolve every issue as soon as it's identified.

Take a hit if you have to, but get it done because your problems never get smaller. Everyone on the team has signed a contract with terms that must be carried out. Delays, design flaws, errors, and client requests all create obstacles to delivering on those contractual obligations--which no one has the time, money, or patience for. Treat every problem or issue as if it's so important it needs to be done yesterday!

## Handshake or Hammer

Providing timely payment to the trades–which has always been a problem–goes a long way toward creating a positive team culture. This is especially true when changes are made, but it's also just good business. Every month, the PM walks the field with the owner and the trade contractors to discuss a completion percentage. That completion percentage goes directly against each contractor's trade payment breakdown.

At the end of each month, those contractors have paid out an exact number of dollars in materials or labor, and they need to be compensated to stay in business. I mentioned previously that cash flow is a matter of life and death in small businesses. Payments should be received within fifteen to thirty days, in my opinion, sixty days max. Trade contracts usually require payment in thirty days, which is fair and allows plenty of time to process payments, but the owner needs to have the correct governance to perform, which is frustratingly uncommon.

When changes are involved, you can incentivize the trades by saying, "We will pay you faster to do something else." There can be some flexibility in these arrangements, all of which can be discussed and agreed upon in the commercial meeting with a handshake.

These details are painstaking but important, because contracts are the basis of how the work gets done; they provide the legal framework for accountability. If you can't fulfill the terms, you shouldn't sign the contract.

The contract also isn't a hammer. It should be a tool to promote goodwill—we all know what we need to do, and we all do it because we want to form a solid professional and personal relationship.

A well-organized, happy team operates this way, and these issues arise very rarely. So do the following:

- Emphasize Project-First Thinking.
- Communicate openly and regularly.
- Work collaboratively to resolve issues.
- Identify and prevent problems so you never have to penalize a contractor.
- Reward contractors for work done well.

The commercial meeting has its place in the system, because inevitably the hammers will come out—even when you've seemingly done everything right. I've sat through countless meetings, week after week, to deal with commercial issues. My most important rule? No one can get personal. You call me something besides my name, the meeting is over for that day.

You can remove a lot of that banging about by focusing on delivery. Deliver good work on schedule, and there's no reason to go to commercial.

## Quality Assurance/Quality Control

QA/QC is the culmination of what I've been writing about. Ideally, it is an attitude that pushes every manager, supervisor, contractor, and trade to keep their eyes open, see a problem when it's small, and then deliver a solution, if possible. If the problem is outside someone's scope of experience or their work assignment, they bring it to the attention of someone who can offer that solution. It's Project-First Thinking; it's collaboration and communication; it's One Team. Shared Success.[sm].

When I was brought into the Global Financial Institution's headquarters renovation, each floor had a punch list of about 7,000 items. The vendor doing the office fronts was responsible for 3,500 items on that list—one trade, half the list! We discovered that the wooden doors had not been properly protected during shipping. We asked why, but all we got in return was "Well, you know."

Well, I didn't. I told them, "If you start protecting your doors, you'll cut out a thousand punch list items." That kind of list wasn't just a one-man-hour problem, and every man-hour cost that vendor $120. It must've cost thousands of dollars to fix in total, and that was insane.

We sat with that vendor and explained the problem to the factory over the phone, insisting that they put cardboard or foam around the doors and tape them up to protect them while in transit. By the end, eliminating the issue of the damaged doors brought the punch list down to between three hundred and four hundred items, one-tenth of the original number. There were other problems besides door finishes, so the contractor went looking for other ways to delete items before they hit the punch list, and they dealt with them.

Why weren't the doors protected from the start? Your guess is as good as mine, but the fact that they weren't was creating extra work for us, so we addressed it. This is what happens when you reprogram the quality assurance team from after-action inspectors to a quality control team of real-time problem seeker-solvers. If something came from the factory wrong, we went to the factory and changed their behavior. When issues stemmed from something done on the jobsite, we worked in the field to encourage better behavior. Maybe we'll never reach the ultimate QA/QC experience—jobs where you have no punch lists—but we need to strive for that goal on every job.

The Global Financial Institution's headquarters project was intended to be a 2-million-square-foot, two-year, $280-million renovation. After four years, all the bad attitudes, mistakes, and oversights had led to a building that was only half-done and over budget by around $80 million. As the first million square feet was built out, the team probably did everything wrong that they could do wrong. Do those mistakes need to be repeated in the second million? If we didn't overhaul the culture on the team, they probably would have been.

As you may recall, we had to bring the architect back in, because they know the vision and intent of that building better than anyone else. The drawings were done the way they were for good reason. We were on the ground, though, and after a few weeks or months, we began to see little tweaks we could make to better reach that intent. There's no one better than the architect to explain that to a carpenter or electrician.

"I want that light here. I know the drawing shows it there, but let's put it here so it lines up better with this. You haven't installed it yet, so we don't have to spend any extra money. Just put it here."

That's an analysis that led to a communication that created a collaboration—not a change order—that improved the dream.

A tradesperson could have said, "You know what? It shows wrong on the drawing, but I have to build it that way by contract, so I will. If they don't like it, they can tell me, and then they can pay me extra to go back and fix it later." That mindset costs somebody money, maybe the client, maybe the electrician, maybe everybody—and it serves no one. "Measure twice, cut once," they say, but we know it's more than that. You must look at everything with a critical eye, learn to see things that might go wrong, improve things the whole way through, and help people to do the same in their jobs.

## Failure to Manage

Looking back over my career, the overly ambitious baggage system really was my biggest challenge. It was certainly the largest commercial issue I've ever experienced, but that project pushed me in an important way. The airport was designed in the 1980s to serve a large city and opened in 1994. During its construction, I was juggling more change orders than I could count, averaging about $1 million per day. On top of that, I had uncovered a total backlog running near $250 million. Dealing with those changes to the original airport plan became my whole life for eighteen months, and I was intent on resolving them fairly.

There were over a hundred prime contractors (GC/CM) and over a thousand trade contractors, which meant a lot of negotiations. I put a special operations group in place to manage them all.

The airport had invited small, minority-owned contractor firms to do much of the work, but because the airport representatives were used to dealing with government agencies and large businesses, nobody had thought through the unique needs of the small businesses they were honestly trying to help.

Many of those businesses didn't have the cash flow to wait for payment while the bureaucratic wheels turned, especially when changes were added to the balance sheets. It sometimes took six months for those changes to be negotiated. They got the work done, often spending a lot of money on labor and materials, but were not promptly paid. The payout schedule became such a serious problem that the project probably put many of those small firms out of business.

Money had become an obstacle, rather than a reward. So in comes the special operations group–thirty-five staffers working only on change order negotiations and estimating.

We asked the airport, "What's going on over here? You've got all these people complaining about money, and you're sitting here holding it back. We have to figure out a way to get these businesses paid." We worked with them to develop a new agreement: once the group negotiated a number, the contractor would be paid 50 percent up front, to take care of their costs, and the rest on completion and acceptance.

With that in place, the focus of the group turned to the trades. We said to each one, "Listen, you have one hundred change orders out there. Which ones are most important to you? Let's start there."

Of course, they responded with the big-ticket items they wanted to be completed and paid for as soon as possible. So, we began clearing out that backlog, negotiating with each trade. We had discussed the airport's ceiling price while developing the new payment agreement, so if the trade was negotiating for a number under that ceiling, we had the authority to approve it right there. Meetings that concluded with an on-the-spot approval were great for everybody!

Our attitude was straightforward. "If you can do this, we can do this, and we have a deal." That approach changed the flavor of the job, and those lingering list items were taken care of.

In the end, the total cost for the airport project came to over $4 billion–probably $2.5 billion in original construction and an additional $500 million in change orders. A 20 percent increase in the final construction cost for changes is ridiculously large. Plus, these figures don't include the cost of the land and other soft costs, so who knows what the final tab really was.

Billing may not sound like a QA/QC issue, but ultimately, everything is, because QA/QC is about how well you do every aspect of the work. QA/QC is based on a simple premise: problems arise and when we find ways to solve them, everybody profits. We may need to look for innovative, nontraditional approaches, but we rarely find problems that have no resolution. By the way, when you have twelve thousand people working on a project, as we did during the last year for the airport project, you can imagine what kinds of problems can arise.

So, here's the $500-million question: how many of those changes could've been prevented? That, sadly, we'll never know with certainty, but I'm sure many of them could've been.

This project was something of a perfect storm--a bureaucracy the size of a major metropolitan government as the client, with an essentially unlimited power to tax and bond to finance the money needed to cover the price tag. The point remains that changes at any scale can turn a profitable project into a disaster. The difference is prevention.

## The Worst-Case Scenario

I mentioned the Global Financial Institution's headquarters renovation, by comparison, had an initial $280 million budget. When I joined the project, the delays and changes to-date had cost them an additional $80 million. Different figures, sure, but the very same problem: quality.

There were very well-known, capable engineers and architects on the job, but the contractors were indifferent to the quality of the work. For any project -- construction or otherwise -- indifference is your worst nightmare. The punch list was forty thousand items long for four floors, and the Institution was moving people in. They should have been handing out hard hats for executives to wear at their desks.

In most cases, a punch list item is an error made by the contractor-- the wrong materials, dents in the wall, crooked corners, or anything that doesn't meet contract specifications. Given the Institution's prestigious reputation, the wall finishes for the C-Suite floors were specified to be Level 5--the best, most detail-oriented, and most expensive work that we do in construction. A long punch list is a huge problem--a work-that-needs-redoing problem after the work is supposedly completed. On the C-Suite floors, any mistakes were going to cost several times as much to correct.

The first floor that I became responsible for was 67,000 square feet and had 7,000 punch list items -- an average of one mistake every 9.6 square feet.

Multiply that by the price of back-tracking each square foot of space and redoing it to the standard specified. At that rate, you're basically building the entire floor twice. This is, more or less, exactly what was happening, because the contractors, and seemingly everyone else, were indifferent to the quality of the work being done. No wonder the project was only half complete at the end of the estimated four years; that's the cost of a punch list–100 percent wasted time and money.

One of the incentives in my contract with the Institution was to reduce the punch list, which required that I shift the team's approach to proactively addressing the mistakes. I asked the general contractor, "How about we actively engage the engineers and architects during the construction process and have them do quality control during the build?"

As I described before, we did it by flipping quality assurance from an afterthought to real-time quality control. I told the architects and engineers, "I want you to walk the field. You see something, tell that trade contractor there's a problem, be it 'This is crooked' or 'That's not the level of finish I need.' Tell them specifically what works and what isn't done right. Then I want you to write it down. Stick a piece of paper on the wall with the stuff you're seeing. Keep a list of every problem and its location. Next time you come around, you'll check it off the list if it's been fixed."

The punch list dove. The tradesman started thinking, "I know how to do this right, and the architect is directly behind me, watching what I'm doing. There's no excuse to do it wrong, and I'm expected to meet the contracted quality. I have to work to the architect's expectation."

On the second floor, we got the list down to 3,500, and the next floor to about 2,000. By the time the last floor was completed, we were down to about 1,000 punch list items. We didn't change how quality was assessed, just when in the process it was evaluated.

In construction, the architects and engineers should do the punch list. That's their proper role, to represent the client's interests, and

I've never seen a contract that forced architects and engineers to wait until the end of the job to make sure those interests were served.

Managers and supervisors can fill this role in many different business settings. If the template for a deck is wrong, the whole presentation will be. If the research is outdated, the strategy won't work. Align your team around your expectations for the delivery up front, show them exactly how you want it done, and then let them execute.

## Errors, Omissions, and Corrections

If you put an architect or engineer—or supervisor or manager—in charge of quality, someone still needs to provide broader oversight. If the contractor runs into a change order that's required because there was a design error or omission, that needs to be *captured* and recorded. The standard of quality for any drawings, plans, templates, and guidelines is the same as the executed work.

In this business, the record of errors and omissions allows you to go back to the architect or engineer and recoup the cost of their mistakes. I'll show them the list and say, "Here's what I'm seeing, and clearly, these are mistakes. They shouldn't have happened, and the owner is paying the extra costs of fixing them."

They usually take care of it. The record shows, specifically, what mistakes happened, and once they understand their errors, architects generally don't repeat them. I've only been involved in suing an architect once, because it was a big change, and the client insisted. They returned about a quarter of a million dollars, but I really don't like to handle things this way.

I prefer to identify and mitigate the problem or issue and resolve it before there is a delay or a cost to the project. *Always* include the architect and engineer in the proposed solution.

## Prevention

I am reminded of an old saying, "It costs you nothing to fix a mistake that never gets made."

In a commercial building, 60 percent of mechanical work goes in between the drop ceiling and the floor above it. If you don't test the equipment while the systems are being built—if you wait until the end—you won't be able to easily access anything because there will be other trades underfoot, literally! You have to do things in an orderly process, system by system. Put the sprinkler pipe in, then check it. Put the HVAC ducts in, then check them. Put the hot water in, put the cold water in, then check them, and so on, until everything is in and done, and you *know* they're done. Install those pipes in an order based on a design. Make sure that every pipe is in the right place and that the valves are accessible. Then, move on to the next step.

These things are vital to the owner who has to operate that building for the next several years or decades. With today's computer models, you can more easily see where everything goes, down to small fractions of an inch. No piping or ductwork should ever interfere with any others. The valves should be accessible for the operations staff to maintain them. When the first trade puts a pipe in the ceiling, the project manager must know *by visual inspection* that it went in right. If it's wrong, the PM must have the trade fix it right then and there—don't let it continue.

If you've been paying attention, you know the contractor should never respond with, "I'm putting it in according to drawing."

Like the project schedule, the drawings are created before anything is put in place and go through a number of changes before construction begins.

The architects and designers start with initial plans for all the systems to be installed. Then they meet, coordinate, and collaborate with the owners, operators, and trades. They review the owner's needs, the operations people weigh in on where things should go, and all the trades share their thoughts. What initially looked good to the architect or designer often ends with them saying, "Yeah, you're right. It probably would be better over there," and the drawings get adjusted. Once the plans are coordinated and signed off, trades can install everything knowing there's proper space for all their equipment.

Quality in mechanical installation isn't just a matter of whether or not the lights come on when you flip the switch. Let's say, throughout the building, outlet covers are being attached crooked. The electrical contractor just goes along not caring, screws it in, and moves to the next one. When the whole job is completed, there could be as many as four thousand crooked outlet covers.

There's another old saying, "How you do anything is how you do everything." It's a good standard. If you catch the poor install quality on one of the first few, you can say, "Listen, those are crooked. We don't accept crooked. This is the intent of our drawings. It's got to be straight. Please, put them on straight." The electrical contractor will have a handful of covers to correct, rather than thousands.

## Result

Often, as you've read, the problem is no more complex than people just aren't talking to each other.

When I asked the engineering guys and architectural crews on the Global Financial Institution project to switch from QA to QC, they were a little bit uncomfortable with the idea. Not surprisingly, it was new, and people don't like to change the way they've always done things. We expected that because we'd feel the same way. Even so, we insisted and waited.

After three months, they were so thrilled with the amount of work they were avoiding that they felt we could do away with punch lists all together. Sadly, not possible—mistakes still get made, but we can cut them down by 50 percent or 75 percent or even 90 percent in some cases.

Yet, I continue to be amazed that there are still people who just don't get it.

I had a supervisor on an airport project whose work became a great example and a selling point for this idea. The supervisor had finished 1 million square feet of space with five hundred punch list items. The Global Financial Institution had one punch list item for about ten square feet of work; this supervisor had one item for every two thousand square feet. How did that happen?

That supervisor oversaw each step every day and wasn't shy about telling the contractors, "Don't do that." Sometimes, it was a single trade; other times, it was a contractor with a pattern of problems. "That's a punch list item, and you're going to have a million of those if you don't start turning it around today" was the mantra on that job.

The contractor doesn't want that million, so an inquiry is made: "Okay, what do you want me to do?"

"I want you to do it this way. It's not much different from what you're doing now, you just need to pay close attention to details. We're looking at these little things."

Speaking of details, I casually mentioned two old proverbs:

- God is in the details.
- The Devil is in the details.

Still seems contradictory, right? Not in construction. Define "God" as "the best work we can do" and "the Devil" as "delays that destroy profits" —quality results or work that must be done over.

I also mentioned that the expectations for what quality needs to be established at the beginning. Remember the architect for the Global Financial Institution headquarters that didn't know what "level 5 finish" meant? The architect inspected and failed the walls, saying they weren't level 5 when they were. They knew quality was expected but didn't really know what it looked like.

In the real world, field conditions require some allowances. If you're building a new wall to meet an existing wall, there could be a little bump, and that isn't a reason to rip the wall out. There's going to be a little bump, and we have to live with it.

In this case, the architect hadn't been properly trained on wall finishes, so the Gypsum Association trained them. We don't expect to see that mistake again.

No one—not even you!—is immune to mistakes. Our best work means everybody is willing to find and mitigate those mistakes while preventing future missteps.

When it comes time for the final inspection, I "take the train." Behind me and the other inspectors will be a cleaner, a painter, a spackler, someone with a screwdriver, someone else with a hammer, all lined up. If we go into a room and see errors, the train runs around quickly to straighten them out before they can end up on the punch list. For a single day's pay for those few people, we might knock out 50 percent of all those potential punch list items.

Action like that sets an example and gets people thinking, They insist we minimize our punch lists, and they're helping us do that. We make it as easy as possible to deliver quality, and the team on the Institution's headquarters delivered!

That first big test of the framework that is now One Team. Shared Success.[sm], the focus on delivery, resulted in about a 50 percent improvement in project performance!

# CHAPTER 10

# The Evolution of One Team. Shared Success.ˢᵐ The Third Step: Tools and Analytics

## Tools

Tools and analytics are the third cornerstone of One Team. Shared Success.ˢᵐ

The analytics piece should be your first clue, but I'm not talking about tactical tools like hammers and drills-- though, those do keep the project moving in the right direction. I'm referring to the collection of data points, or key performance indicators (KPIs), that allow you to measure and track progress.

KPIs are important on any project in any business. In construction, they're one of the ways you get paid, but the numbers are more than that; they help us identify problem areas and promote collaboration, contributing to team culture. They help us deliver quality, ensuring our effectiveness. Most importantly, they keep us keyed to delivery.

Determining which numbers and tools to use and how to use them requires the work of qualified, experienced people.

I mentioned before that the role of the construction manager (CM) was initially designed to serve as the owner's eyes and ears on the job, overseeing and directing the trade contractors performing the work. The CM, sometimes referred to as a master builder (MB) or construction specialist (CS), is a key player on the team, the person who really knows how to build stuff. This isn't a friend trusted to look out for the owner's interests, and it isn't a project manager in training.

It's a builder with extensive experience planning and executing the exact sequence of events as they need to happen on the jobsite; they've got it all in their head, and they need to put it on paper

Everything the CM does is about getting the trades, equipment, and materials on site when they're needed and getting the tasks done when they need to be done so that the next task can get started on schedule or before.

The CM needs to share resources with the owner's team or a separate resource who works for the owner directly to make sure things are going the way they should. Who goes first, who goes second, and who goes third? Everything must be built in a sequence, because if not, we end up tearing out work done properly to redo work done improperly. That sequence is the basis of the project schedule. Delays are where unnecessary costs are incurred, where profits are lost and schedules—including the owner's scheduled opening and occupancy—go all to hell. Having real expertise based on real experience makes sure that all those activities happen smoothly.

## Proactive Scheduling

Project management is, more than anything, proper scheduling properly executed.

Scheduling, however, is probably one of the most misused and abused systems on any project.

As a result, CMs and builders generally don't use the schedule as a management process or a reporting tool in our industry, and they miss out on a lot of its potential. The methodology of One Team. Shared Success.[sm] disrupts this mindset, instead making the schedule the first and last thing the team looks at each day.

My first job out of college in 1978 was for a big company that built petrochemical plants. Back then, they called scheduling EPC—engineer, procure, and construct; today, EPC is known as design-build.

The architects designed the plant, arranging everything where it needed to be on paper. We built based on that design, and each of our activities were tied to fees. I was responsible for reporting exactly what work was performed each month, i.e. how much material we installed. There were specified unit rates for each type of material–the cost of a twelve-inch pipe versus an eight-inch pipe, for example--as well as standards for things like the number of man-hours required to install each foot of pipe. These benchmarks were tracked to determine overall productivity performance.

At the end of each month, our total fee was based on the amount of productivity relative to *one*-- the amount of work scheduled for that month. The schedule, as it had been agreed upon, was the prime KPI. If productivity was less, say, 0.9, the team still got paid, but less than the maximum possible rate because the activities completed fell short of the schedule expectations.

That job illustrated the need to be effective in scheduling and production, because *we were measured*. Questions were asked, and answers were given. We did the work, and we got paid according to that work.

It's universal and well accepted in business that "performance measured is performance improved." My first experience of a project schedule was its use as a unit of measurement for performance--a tool--but I learned that it's more commonly used as a report, and in some cases, a weapon.

Everyone on the team would get a schedule, and the client would get a schedule, but the progress reports weren't delivered until fifteen to twenty days after the end of the month. At that point, the information is useless. Whatever activities the reports described happened two or more weeks ago; those numbers have zero value.

One Team. Shared Success.ˢᵐ requires the use of *proactive scheduling*. The proactive schedule drives the project forward, and decades of experience demonstrate it's a winning program. If the schedule is prepared properly, it outlines all the activities that must take place.

It's a blueprint for how to do the work, which is as valuable as the blueprint that shows what work is to be done.

The schedule is full of actionable data—indicators of success and failure—if you know how to use them.

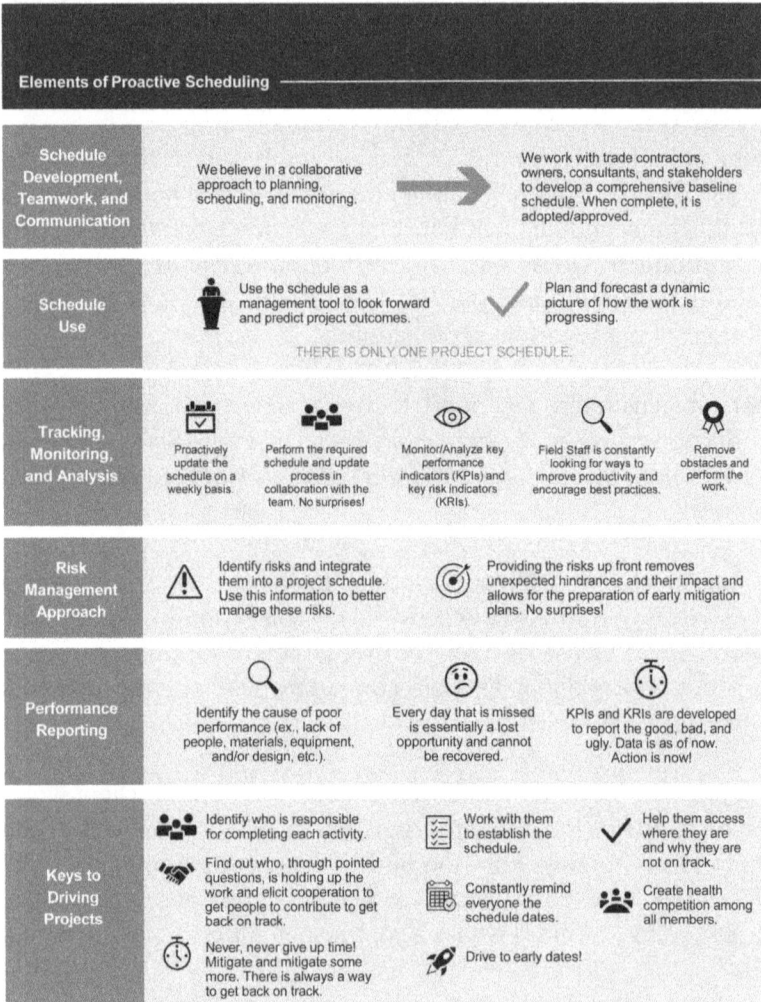

**Elements of Proactive Scheduling**

| | | |
|---|---|---|
| **Schedule Development, Teamwork, and Communication** | We believe in a collaborative approach to planning, scheduling, and monitoring. | We work with trade contractors, owners, consultants, and stakeholders to develop a comprehensive baseline schedule. When complete, it is adopted/approved. |
| **Schedule Use** | Use the schedule as a management tool to look forward and predict project outcomes. | Plan and forecast a dynamic picture of how the work is progressing. THERE IS ONLY ONE PROJECT SCHEDULE. |
| **Tracking, Monitoring, and Analysis** | Proactively update the schedule on a weekly basis. / Perform the required schedule and update process in collaboration with the team. No surprises! / Monitor/Analyze key performance indicators (KPIs) and key risk indicators (KRIs). / Field Staff is constantly looking for ways to improve productivity and encourage best practices. / Remove obstacles and perform the work. | |
| **Risk Management Approach** | Identify risks and integrate them into a project schedule. Use this information to better manage these risks. | Providing the risks up front removes unexpected hindrances and their impact and allows for the preparation of early mitigation plans. No surprises! |
| **Performance Reporting** | Identify the cause of poor performance (ex., lack of people, materials, equipment, and/or design, etc.). / Every day that is missed is essentially a lost opportunity and cannot be recovered. / KPIs and KRIs are developed to report the good, bad, and ugly. Data is as of now. Action is now! | |
| **Keys to Driving Projects** | Identify who is responsible for completing each activity. / Find out who, through pointed questions, is holding up the work and elicit cooperation to get people to contribute to get back on track. / Never, never give up time! Mitigate and mitigate some more. There is always a way to get back on track. | Work with them to establish the schedule. / Constantly remind everyone the schedule dates. / Drive to early dates! / Help them access where they are and why they are not on track. / Create health competition among all members. |

Proactive Schedule Development and Management

**Requests for Information**

One trigger point for scheduling is a request for information (RFI). If a contractor doesn't understand the design when he's installing something, it's written up as an RFI to get clarity on how to best execute. There's usually a two-week window allotted to answer the RFI, so any progress on that installation is stalled. As part of the team reorganization process, I had the engineer attend the delivery meetings to discuss any of those RFIs and get the quickest resolution for the contractor.

The same goes for the architect. When these players are present, we can quickly work through any confusion about the designs. Sometimes it's as simple as, "No, the drawing is clear; you just need to do it this way." Other times, we might discover a design flaw; the engineer sees it, gets an explanation of why it's wrong, and again, we can fix it right there and move on. If the engineers and architects aren't attending these delivery meetings, I've seen it take months to completely answer and resolve an RFI.

Obviously, this process causes delays, but it can also affect claims. Some contractors will rack up a bunch of RFIs and then submit a claim for added payment. If, instead, they're meeting weekly with the people who designed the project and they fail to use that opportunity to address any questions, they will certainly lose that claim.

One Team. Shared Success.™ puts a system in place to prevent RFIs from bogging the project down; they are logged when submitted and put on the next delivery meeting agenda, the resolution is documented, and action is taken accordingly.

**Submittals**

When a design calls for something specific—a type of stone, a species of wood, or even a light with a certain wattage—the contractor must submit a sample of what they intend to procure for the architect's approval. Once the selection has been approved, the contractor can purchase the material. This process is intended to safeguard against ordering and wasting money on the wrong materials, especially for custom items that can't be returned. It's hardly foolproof.

Submittals get stalled or changed all the time. The contractor may misunderstand the intent of that submittal and send a sample to the architect that doesn't meet the stated requirements. If the architect doesn't catch it, we now have a product being delivered that's been authorized but doesn't actually meet the contract. What happens then?

Sometimes you have to stop and replace everything. Other times, you just have to make it work. These situations must be handled with tact, courtesy, and professionalism because what's been put on the wall or installed elsewhere is what you'll have when you finish the job.

Like RFIs, each submittal should be logged, discussed, and approved with all possible speed. If ten submittals have been sitting on the agenda for a month, the CM or PM has to step in and say, "Listen, we've got to spend the next meeting on clearing submittals. Stop other things, and let's get this done!"

Once a submittal is sent, the decision passes from the contractor to management—which could include the CM, PM and/or the owner—for final review. Management must proactively approve submittals because, until that happens, nothing gets ordered. Maintaining engaged leadership on the project helps to keep this process streamlined.

## Financials

All the RFIs and submittals, as well as all change orders and claims, affect the budget. Every issue costs money to resolve and execute. Those financial records can be great indicators of where the problem areas lie and where you're really doing well. How many change orders are sitting out there? How many have been approved versus how many rejected? How many RFIs have been submitted? How many have been resolved? How long did it take? Too many charges in any given department may indicate leadership problems.

Using the financials as a tool to help identify trends and resolve problems saves money—and in most cases, will also accelerate delivery.

### Accountability

Proactive scheduling works because it creates accountability.

Every activity has a person assigned to it:
- This name is tattooed on this activity. This person is responsible for starting this activity on this day and for finishing it on this day.
- That name is tattooed on that next activity. That person is responsible for starting that next activity on that day and finishing it on that day.
- And so, right down the line, task after task.

You've all heard this: "There is no 'I' in 'team.'" Technically true, but in practice, there are a lot of "I"s in "team"–individuals, each of whom need to be held responsible for what they do.

Delivery is tied to performance, and all performances must be tied to individual team members. That performance is reviewed every week by the CM and the team and determines what was completed–not as a report, but as a tool to understand the progress made and how it relates to tasks not yet done:

Do we have a delay? How do we change the schedule to accommodate that delay? Have all the materials been delivered? Did we have enough people on site? What new trades are coming in next week? Are we completely out of their way? Since this task finished early, are we ready to start the next task early?

## Organization

I mentioned that people who don't take schedules seriously, or think of them as meaningless reports, underestimate their power as a management tool in maintaining the first two cornerstones of One Team. Shared Success.sm, alignment and organization, after they've been set. This is especially true for managing resources -- both human and material.

When a task is added to the schedule, the correct quantities of materials required to complete that task are built backwards into the schedule to ensure they arrive on time for the work of a given day. Let's say, you're supposed to pour ten yards of concrete today. You can track that concrete, and you need to--carefully. Many materials can sit on a jobsite for a day or a week, if they've arrived early, which can be helpful if you're targeting early start dates. Ready-to-pour concrete, however, cannot sit around. You have to get it to the right spot at the right time or the load might become useless. Almost without exception, that's a preventable failure.

People--the labor--must also be built into the schedule. Remember, it's your team that gets you from the dream to a finished project. If the task or tasks need seventy-five people to execute on this day, and fifty show up, only two-thirds of the work--at best--will get done, and that's assuming all the other factors went right. If you aren't using the schedule as a proper tool, the likelihood of that is slim.

These numbers are all actionable data points; they tell you how activities must be sequenced and what's required to complete them to make way for next week's work. These are tools that everybody can use to set, manage, and maintain the pace of proactive scheduling.

I've emphasized that One Team. Shared Success.$^{sm}$ framework provides a time and place for everything, and the schedule is no different; it's the backbone of the operation. Begin with the baseline schedule, the best-case scenario. Then add in the resources needed--materials, permits and inspections, utilities, personnel--and of course, a little leeway for the unavoidable delays, like weather, earthquakes, and the occasional horde of locusts. Every layer is outlined, and everything has its place, on paper, for the CM to review every week.

## Collaboration and Communication

Proactive scheduling also plays a role in the team's ability to work best together. If leadership is using it as the tool it can be, it can go a long way in creating a collaborative atmosphere--the "happy" worksite I wrote about earlier.

Once the "culture killers" have been removed from the management team, the team members that remain must find a way to genuinely work together. Some personalities naturally tend to look at their part of a project as their private kingdom, and they see any inquiry about their work as though it were an invasion. Others simply aren't used to this idea and are reluctant to change. Either problem can be destabilizing, but both can be overcome with courtesy, respect, and a positive example.

Committees have had a well-deserved, bad reputation for centuries. "If Moses had been a committee," the old joke says, "the Israelites would still be in Egypt." When a group gets together, people can hide behind the group—anonymity breeds avoidance of responsibility. That's where a good CM can become a great CM. A great CM takes charge, lays down the rules as to how the team is going to conduct business, and sticks to the agenda, insisting that each member of the team contributes.

- Who's telling their story every week? Every team member.
- How do you get everybody to open up? You ask specific questions and then stop talking until you get an answer.
- What questions do you ask?
  - "What are you doing next week?"
  - "What are your needs for those tasks?"
- What answers do you get?
  - "I'm going to be on this task on this floor."
  - "I need these people to be out of my way on this floor."
  - "We're out of stock on this, that, and the other thing. When can I get a delivery of more material?"
  - "I'm behind on these tasks. Can I get 10 extra people for the week to catch up?"

I have been amazed by some projects, like the Global Financial Institution's headquarters, with how tough those seemingly simple ideas can be to achieve. Having a set system in place makes it easier.

Proactive scheduling is a series of formal communications you have every week, and informal communications you might have daily in preparation for that weekly meeting. Through the development and evolution of the One Team. Shared Success.ˢᵐ approach, we created a proprietary tool for this which talks about the pieces: Schedule development, schedule use, monitoring, maintenance and analysis, risk management, and performance reporting. That feedback, distributed to everybody involved, allows the team to see a clear picture of what's happening on that project.

If you can control the necessary communications, you will be very successful.

Those "monitoring" conversations also allow you to see when something isn't not going well and shift into risk management mode. A risk to any one task—safety issue, delay, any problem—is a risk to the entire project. The earlier that risk is identified, the more likely you can resolve it while it's small, allowing the project to continue running as smoothly as possible.

To effectively review the data, you have to make a record on paper or in an electronic file. Remember:

- "If it's not written down, it didn't happen."
- "The weakest pencil (or tablet) is more powerful than the strongest memory."
- "If the pen is mightier than the sword, the word processor should be covered under the START Treaty."

How can we get everybody on the same page if we don't have any pages? Collaboration and alignment require that everybody has agreed to the plan and knows their place in it. When a project is running on an accelerated schedule—before I finalize that document—I'll call every vendor into a room, sit down, and talk about who goes first, who goes second, why this is the order, and what the expectations are. The schedule allows me to say, "On Tuesday, the twelfth, at seven a.m., you've got to be here to do your thing." That date might be two months off, but that level of detail is essential when the timeline is accelerated.

It works. This process results in a minimum of shutdowns, delays, and other problems. I once renovated a two-thousand-square-foot dental clinic in two weeks, because every team member had their game time and was fully prepared when that moment was up. They knew I would be calling the day before and asking them, "Are you going to be here?" I knew each of them would say, "Yes." Everybody was waiting, and everybody took on the responsibility to be successful. I won't say it's never been done like that before, I'm sure it has, but I was proud of how smoothly and quickly that project fell into place.

In addition to effective scheduling, I think the project also benefited from the creation of a little healthy competition. We got people who wanted to outperform each other in a fun way. I've always tried to do that in subsequent jobs.

In 1995, we had been hired by an airport authority's design-build team to turn around a $150-million automated passenger-mover system project. When we came aboard, three associates and I rebuilt the schedule.

We completely overhauled and owned every phase of it, meeting weekly with all the key people. Among them, one person was overseeing systems, the other track work, and another train controls. We started reminding every superintendent and foreman that their names were in the schedule against certain activities. Every week, each of them would come into the meeting, one at a time, and talk about their progress.

They came in for the first meeting of the first month and reported lost man-hours. In fact, they'd lost around a thousand work hours in a month. I told them I expected them to catch up.

They asked, "How do we do that?"

They were understandably upset with me for making such a demand. But in the second month, one supervisor walked into the room, strutting like a peacock, and said, "I'm a thousand work hours ahead of schedule this month."

Now, it was my turn to ask, "How did you do that?"

That supervisor said, "Well, I figured out what you were trying to do. I went to the trade in front of me, the one who was responsible for putting the steel up. I need to hang my conduit on that steel, and I had that trade put them up a few days early. I got started a few days early and all activities accelerated."

I could have kissed that supervisor. Don't worry, I didn't.

They all came in about a month later, thinking, "How do I beat this thing? I'm not physically getting beaten up, but it feels like it to walk into that meeting a thousand or two thousand work hours behind."

Eventually, they figured it out. After a year, those trades completed the monorail a week early. A light had gone on in one person's head, which led to lights in other heads. I didn't tell that trade; I just led a little bit, and they figured it out. That trade got the trade that followed to accelerate at no added cost.

People are motivated most when they want to get things done; they're either motivated when the project begins—that's the simple way—or they allow everything to fall apart and run late, forcing everybody to scramble to meet their deadlines so they get their bonuses. That's a recipe for disaster—shoddy workmanship and punch list items. The critical path method is this: "I've got to figure out a way to make this better because the other way doesn't work."

Likewise, if these activities slip, you risk this much time and this much profit down the road, so it's best for everyone to get the activities done on time. Each task always affects other tasks—one change leads to more changes. Instead, put healthy competition into play, and watch people gain pride. They want to do things better because then they can brag about it. When you manage expectations like that, you set everybody up for success.

## Give People Room to Succeed

Once you have the right atmosphere established on a worksite, you can let people do what they need to do.

Our team once did a renovation with a mechanical problem—twenty air handlers to be replaced. Air handlers are big fans that push air through the ductwork. At no point in the first year of the project did anyone mention getting those replaced. Finally, we told the contractor, "You have twenty of those to replace, and now you have just twelve months to do it. You can't take them all out of service at the same time, because they have to feed air into the building. So you have to stage each one of those in a way that keeps the building fed with air while replacing all of them."

When I did that, the contractor told me, "I've been trying to do that for two years now, but they wouldn't let me do it."

"Who wouldn't let you do it?"

"Well, the CM that was in charge at the time."

"Well, that CM is gone. This is your field. Get it done."

That contractor had been pushed into a near-impossible situation by their own actions. Now they had to get themselves out of it. Conventional wisdom said that each air handler would take something around two months to remove and replace. That was twice as much time as we had. We backed that contractor up to the wall, and they finally understood: "I've got to move. I've got to get going on these."

The data said it was almost impossible to make the schedule at that point. We worked out a detailed, modified schedule with that contractor and ensured they understood so well that they'd follow it like they were born to. They knew it was the last thing that had to get done to get that building open, and they got it done.

## Technology

How can we improve the delivery by speeding processes up? Integrating the schedule with new technology is one way.

We use workforce-counting software by which we collect data electronically. Everybody who walks through the gate gets tagged, which allows us to track their data. We know that worker's name, what trade they belong to, what company employs them, as well as what time that worker entered and left every day. We have notes telling us about the expected productivity for the day, and we track actual performance every day. This makes those weekly meetings much simpler.

We also have 4-D modeling software in which you can virtually model the project on screen with its schedule. Whenever you update the schedule, the software shows it on the screen visually. When you put a structure on a large-screen monitor like that, everybody can look at what has to go into that structure. It can lead to some interesting situations. When I worked at the petrochemical plant—that first job out of college—there was some major equipment that had to go in very early on. The doors simply weren't going to be big enough to allow the equipment to be brought in after they were installed, so we built one or two floors then stacked that equipment and continued the build around it. Visualization allows you to understand little details like that—which are not, after all, little details—so things can move faster and more effectively.

## Focus

### Analysis and Correction

Constant attention to the schedule facilitates improved performance. I've mentioned before, a professional schedule includes key performance indicators (KPIs)—specific checkpoints you can use to judge performance and success and prevent risks.

## Reinforcing Progress

How does the effective use of tools and analytics fit into the overarching message of team collaboration and shared success across the project cycle?

An old sage once said, "History is the proof of the theory."

My schedule says I'm going to do this and that. My analytics say I got it done. Every activity is a goal–all have scope, duration, and logic. Each of those things serves as a KPI. All of them, stacked up, aligned, and connected constitute the schedule. With that schedule set, everybody has committed to getting things done, and there's a methodology to monitor that. This got done on time, and that got done on time. Subconsciously, people begin to understand that this or that behavior is right, because it's effective. Everybody feels good about getting things done on time, and they go all out to repeat that feeling.

To be effective, the schedule, the analytics, and the KPIs, must all be realistic. This is why you need a master builder––or master orchestrator––in charge of it; you need someone with the experience and skill set to phase it out appropriately. Their main goal must be to create a situation in which we're all helping others. "No man is an island," that old poet said.[12] We emphasize that each worker is part of a team, and each team is part of the big team. Self-reliance is an admirable attitude until it says, "I don't need anybody." When, instead, if people start singing, "He ain't heavy, he's my brother," amazing things happen.[13]

---

[12] John Donne, "XVII. Meditation," *Devotions Upon Emergent Occasions, and Several Steps in my Sickness* [sic], 1624. Often published in a poetic format, read the entire passage at: https://www.poemhunter.com/poem/no-man-is-an-island/, accessed 25 January 2024.

[13] Bobby Scott and Bob Russell, "He Ain't Heavy, He's My Brother," from the album *Defunct* by Kelly Gordon, Capitol Records, 1969.

## Excuses

Another quote worth noting, "There's always a reason and always an excuse—and whenever there's an excuse, you probably won't like the reason."

That vendor who was shipping doors without padding probably had the best of intentions —perhaps thinking everybody would save money on shipping, but even that is nothing but an excuse for poor judgment. Any added shipping cost would've been far less than the cost of fixing those damaged doors.

We encountered a similar, but different, challenge on a project with a trade responsible for radiator covers. That trade wouldn't make them until the wall was built. We said, "Wait a second, the walls are already there on the drawing. You know how long each cover should be."

"But that's not the real wall," the trade replied, which was actually a reasonable recognition that changes or variations can be made from the drawing to the finished product—a scenario I've outlined has happened a few times, in fact. The trade insisted that pre-building the covers would inevitably result in a lot of change orders, requiring that all the work be done over. Not unlike the desire to save on shipping costs, this is a legitimate fear and a reasonable plan for saving money. Unfortunately, it took six weeks to get radiator covers built, and by waiting for the finished wall to start that build, other things would be delayed.

We had two opposing viewpoints, both technically correct, requiring a little creative thinking. Everybody knew that any deviations from the drawing would be minor, so we suggested: "Subtract a quarter of an inch from the cover, and make a little trim piece or something to cover any gaps."

Little things like that weren't being solved for on that job, and they ended up becoming big issues. Our job was to eliminate them. We told the radiator cover person, "We need the radiator covers, and we expect them on these dates. It's your responsibility to make that happen." The message was received, and they built a little flexibility in the cover sizes. No change orders were submitted, and not one objection to their quality came to our attention.

I mentioned these kinds of people earlier-- the "kings of my little kingdom" people who like to throw stuff in front of you. They take pride in their work, want to be in control of it, and be the most important person on the job. The PM or CM needs to walk through those imaginary gates to the kingdom. Take the facts to them and demand that their performance conforms with the schedule.

I was told off by one of these "kings" on a $750-million railroad station project in a big city. I was walking on the site one day and saw a trade hanging subway tiles in a bathroom. The job was almost done, with just the bottom two rows to go. The work had started at the top, and on those last two rows, a different color and size were being installed. I looked at the installer and said, "Excuse me. Do you recognize that those tiles are the wrong color and size?"

"I get paid to hang the tile. That's what I get paid for," was the reply, and in truth, they got paid the same whether the tile was hung correctly or not. Someone with no regard for the design or the subsequent work that must be done will also accept no responsibility for their mistakes. They'll blame others or ignore their mistakes completely, but that installer's boss would ultimately pay for it to be corrected, and busting out tiles isn't cheap. We discussed this situation with that boss, and they got it fixed.

## Challenges

Some projects involve limitations or expectations that simply have to be met. School rehab construction, as I mentioned, must happen during the summer. We take a classroom out of service on June 1, and by August 20 or 30, that classroom must be ready to serve the students. Without a proactive schedule, we can't pull it off. I've completed $10 million projects in a single summer because I had a step-by-step plan; you cannot mobilize all the things that have to happen otherwise. Every task was updated every week, the whole team knew where the problems were, and everybody contributed to the fixes. The process works, but you simply can't keep it all in your head; no one is that smart. So, get it on the schedule!

A client may have a schedule firmly in mind or the several departments each have separate schedules. I maintain that the best successes only happen on projects with a single schedule. That's not a fun or easy battle, and you only win it by not engaging. I tell them, "I'm not taking this project on unless I have a unified schedule. If not, I'm done and gone. I can't have you with your own schedule reporting on something different than I'm reporting on mine. Separate schedules set us at odds, making communication and collaboration much more difficult, if not impossible. We need one schedule that contains all the documents and all the data necessary to execute this project." That approach works because it's completely non-combative.

If we have multiple schedules being executed, we'll never ever know if we're behind or ahead, because there's only one truth. In fact, our company has what we call the "Record of Truth." Every document, everything we do in our company, goes into that record, even salaries and vacation time. You don't need to go to a payroll company for our data because it's in our salary app. Vacations are in the personnel app. Everything is tracked in the Record of Truth, and it's our proof that our system works. Our books are 100 percent open to our clients. If they don't agree with our schedule, they're welcome to make any comments they want. We'll listen to all the advice, and give it due consideration; if it's valid, we'll use it to update our schedule.

But our projects still have only one schedule, and that schedule is ours.

## Conclusion

The schedule and all of its associated data points help you to develop KPIs that measure progress along the critical path. A "zero float" means you can't delay a task by a day, or you'll delay the whole project by a day--this is more or less an entire project run on late start dates. A "positive float," on the other hand, means you have some wiggle room to delay one task without delaying other tasks. As you've seen, the One Team. Shared Success.ˢᵐ approach encourages trades to get going on the early start dates whenever possible, because starting early means you can finish early. That builds a reserve of completed activities, de-risking the project as it progresses and allowing you to react faster and more effectively to unforeseen conditions/problems, such as when the weather drops an unavoidable delay on you.

KPIs are an important part of Project-First Thinking. We're not protecting anybody; we're protecting everybody. We're reporting the facts and dealing with those facts, harsh or helpful. We report the truth as our data shows it and use it to collaborate with the team in creating and updating a schedule that everybody can engage with and do great things, as a result.

One of those "great things" we do is work ourselves out of a job. Think about it: You win a project, you get a start date, then you do your best and finish a day or a week ahead of schedule. You've just worked yourself out of that job but freed yourself up for a new one. That's the nature of the construction industry, and it's one good way to build a positive reputation.

The retail industry understands this and among their fundamental principles is repeat business. It costs a huge amount of money to win new customers, compared to the cost of winning repeat business.

In our business, you may only deal directly with client A or client B once in your life, but they have friends. If you can walk around a jobsite at completion with a client, and they say, "You did a great job. It was a pleasure doing business with you," you have really succeeded, and they're going to spread the word. I was meeting with a consultant, an architect, some time ago, who spoke glowingly about a project we'd done with the firm. The architect said, "What a great job. During that job, I formed this unbelievable relationship with the project manager, who is now among my best friends." That's not only a great endorsement, but another reason to do good work.

I relayed this conversation to a contractor not long after. "What comes out of this behavior is relationships that last the rest of your life. Because now, you've got people that trust you. Working together, you get stuff done. Your professional connections–and the same is true of personal connections–become part of your team. When that happens, it's not just you looking for your next project, but your whole team (including all your professional connections) is helping you look, because they want to work with you again.

And they'll recommend that others do the same.

The use of these tools and analytics made about a 20 percent improvement in project performance; that's how you get them glowing about you.

# CHAPTER 11

# Advancing Technology

---

Evolving technology has introduced tremendous opportunities for our team to do much more work than we've ever done before, and that progress will continue. The development of AI is accelerating technology like never before. In fact, it's evolving so rapidly that much of the discussion in this book will need to be applied to even newer programs and technologies to continue improving delivery.

People have described my pragmatic and hands-on approach to business as old school. While this may be true, I also consider myself an "early adopter," not one who waits for technology to prove itself before buying in.

In 1984, I bought my first portable PC, a Compaq Portable computer, which was the size of a small suitcase. It was referred to as the Compaq Luggable. Ever since, I've embraced technology as another tool in the belt, rather than shy away from new innovations. This has impacted how I approach the continued improvement of our process: Every time there's something new, I get my people to try it. It's not just about increasing productivity; it's also about how sophisticated the data can be. We run our company using an application that provides high-quality data points, connecting each aspect of our business. We essentially built an enterprise resource planning (ERP) system in Salesforce. We're intentionally tech-savvy; we've been working remotely without issue for fifteen years. We're on the leading edge of that curve, because it provides us with real value; we have the agility to be where we're needed, when we're needed. When the pandemic hit and many workplaces had to work out the kinks as they adjusted to a virtual environment, we were already pros at collaborating with one another that way. As early adopters of that model--and the use of technology in that way--we were prepared when everyone else caught up.

## Lasers

Today, lasers can measure floors and walls among other things, collecting data that can be used with AI to generate blueprints and plans.

That system automates an immense amount of work that would otherwise be done manually but still has limitations. We can scan an existing structure and draw around that data, but AI doesn't see when you install something. The technology can interpret the data better, but the scanning and capturing processes are not automatic. I expect to see AI overcome this limitation someday soon, but until then, we work around it.

Construction is about installation—pipes, ducting, walls, anything. When you know exactly where stuff is and you know the plan, you can tell if you've gotten it right or not. Someday, lasers will be telling us that.

## Video

The use of drones on site can provide an overhead look to indicate progress, logistics, safety, and other problems. There is still some work to do on this front, but it won't be many years to go until drones become a really powerful tool. With this technology, it's possible to capture what's been done, but so far, it isn't able to automatically compare that against what was planned.

As this book was being written, we used a project for a state highway authority as a test. The project included twenty different sites all over the state, meaning we couldn't possibly visit each one every day, which leads us to rely on locals on the ground. If they could fly drones, we could capture actionable data. We'd have proof that tasks were completed with date codes confirming that work was proceeding on schedule. When problems arose, that onsite person could show us what was going on in real time, allowing us to deal with that issue immediately.

Body cameras are increasingly being utilized by construction companies, as well, as they have been valuable tools for law enforcement for years. Their footage not only confirms tasks completed, but can also be valuable in addressing safety issues, reporting inappropriate behavior, providing greater transparency, and demonstrating proper procedures for training purposes.

## Blockchain

Hacking—changing or manipulating data, holding data for ransom, and other problems—is a growing threat to everyone who uses computers...and I mean everyone! Blockchain distributes ledgers or databases, duplicating them across multiple platforms in a way that makes hacking extremely difficult. As long as all the platforms agree, the system knows no hacks have occurred. If one platform is hacked, the others can reject that data and repair it.

I've stressed previously the need to have a single schedule so that everyone is aligned and on the same page--blockchain technology may ensure that everyone is on the *right* page.

## Cryptocurrencies

Bitcoin has thus far been the most popular form of cryptocurrency, but all of them are gaining new users daily. These currencies can be considered more secure than some financial institutions, as they're overseen via blockchain software.

Cryptocurrencies ("cryptos" for short) are digital currency—no physical paper or coin involved. Some people use them to pay for goods and services, while others tend to lean on them as speculation and investment--some do both. The "crypto" part of the name derives from the "cryptographic" techniques that allow people to spend them securely and avoid involvement with governments or banks. The payments are also instantaneous, which would help ensure trades get paid even faster in the future with more widespread adoption.

Already, several major companies accept cryptos—AMC, AT&T, CheapAir, Dish TV, Microsoft, PayPal, Tesla, and *Time* Magazine, to name just a few. Where that's going to go is anyone's guess.

## Artificial Intelligence

Data that exists on all construction sites but are owned by the various parties involved and are not shared openly. We've been working to change that approach in order to eliminate surprises, make informed decisions, and above all, prevent delays.

We rely on relevant key performance indicators (KPIs) and key risk indicators (KRIs) -- what I've been calling "actionable data" -- to provide insights on project performance, promote accountability, and mitigate bad behavior to achieve best value outcomes. AI has the power to transform the entire process by analyzing and ranking data by risk and providing mitigation solutions.

Actionable data feeds can include the following:

- Schedule
- Workforce (manpower)
- Procurement (materials and equipment)
- BIM (Plan, Actual, Quality)
- Safety
- Risks
- Identification and mitigation strategies
- RFIs
- Submittals
- QA/QC - Punch lists
- Financial
  - Potential change orders (Entitlement)
  - Change orders approved to date
  - Rejected change orders
  - Paid to date

○ Contingency usage

Here are example KPIs:

- Planned/actual trade manpower
- Manage to early start dates
- Worker safety
- QA/QC (design compliance)
- Operational effectiveness

Here are examples of KRIs:

- Schedule delays
- Cost overruns
- Quality issues
- Safety incidents
- Contract disputes
- Changes in scope
- Weather events
- Material shortages
- Labor disputes
- Economic conditions

## AI and Data Analysis

All actionable data can be accumulated and analyzed by AI in real time to make informed decisions. The first step is getting access to the data consistently, creating the analysis, and interpreting its findings. I believe this advancement is achievable within the next five years; I've already made strides in getting access to necessary data through my scheduling procedure.

We have a variety of different types of data outlined in those master schedules—construction documents completion, manpower needed, materials and equipment required, permits, utilities, and so on. If we automate the collection and analysis of this data using AI, many existing pain points might be eliminated entirely.

Let's say that, on a particular day, ten people showed up on a job site and you're supposed to have fifteen. If AI is tagging them, you can know by 7:02 a.m. that five people who should've arrived at 7:00 a.m. didn't. The AI can then flag via text, email, or even an automated voice message that outlines the outstanding number of people needed for a task.

We still have humans tracking the schedule, and on large projects, especially, someone might miss the fact that a permit is late. AI could see this scheduling data at one time and warn us, "You cannot proceed with task Y in four days, because the permit for that work is due today and has not arrived."

AI may help us see potential problems faster and more accurately. We constantly ask, "How will that problem impact the overall project schedule?" AI can extrapolate that answer to provide the CM or PM with a fuller, more complete picture (perhaps in minutes instead of hours) and adjust accordingly.

Perhaps we'll soon start to use our data captured by AI to track other things that drag a project down—shipments, weather, vacations, sick days—the list is extensive. This application could make it an effective risk management tool. As of the writing of this book, I have not seen that this sort of software is available, or even possible, but I'm confident that it can be done.

Adding an AI capability to our existing project management software—scanning programs to compare drone footage to scheduled work, for example—could help get things done faster than we can do them today. I've mentioned mechanical systems, which is the most important thing in putting up a building besides the walls, have to be done right, because there's only so much room above the ceiling. There are also many other recurring risks that tend to pop up in virtually every job. Through AI, we might be able to figure out how to remove those risks. I'm sure we'll eventually find a way to ask AI the right questions to boil issues down to a checklist that AI can create and track -- provided a profession is still in charge of ensuring it hasn't hallucinated.

Where manpower is concerned, we constantly ask, "What's the optimum number of people for today's tasks?" Scheduling a multimillion-dollar project makes optimizing manpower needs a major challenge. Can AI do that better or faster than humans?

I believe AI use is going to explode in popularity. We have yet to see how many tasks really can be simplified with it. Once AI is able to generate a return on investment, new software products will become available to make our work more effective and profitable.

A major concern that arises from AI is the technology taking jobs away from humans. Historically, that's a complaint made about robots, computers, and many past new technologies. Yes, that will happen. Once AI starts to perform construction tasks regularly—we're not talking tomorrow, but certainly soon—some jobs will be lost. However, the people who used to build cars that are now being built by robots are now those building and maintaining the robots. People who used to perform accounting tasks by hand are now programming accounting software. It's a really interesting thing to look at from a construction perspective, because you're probably not going to have as many people on a site. Those who are on site will be monitored quite extensively. How will that change the construction industry?

The auto industry hasn't folded up, neither has accounting services, and the economy hasn't crashed from massive unemployment. But "The times they are a-changin'."[14] Construction, one of the slowest adopters of technology, will now continue to change forever. How? Your guess is as good as mine.

## AI and Prevention

Change orders ran rampant on the airport project with the overly ambitious baggage system, leading to delays and $500 million in added costs. Every single time, we had to stop, figure out the details

---

[14] Bob Dylan, "The Times They Are a-Changin'," from the album *The Times They Are a-Changin'* by Bob Dylan, Columbia Recording, 1965.

of the change, rework the design drawings, and negotiate with contractors if there were to be added costs associated with those changes. I did that by checking manually, and it consumed my life for nearly two years. I reviewed all of the change orders and why those changes occurred. For that one engineer on the Texas highway project, I found an error designed into every project they had worked on.

AI also has the potential to search through data to find out where things go wrong and why. With this capability, I might be able to go to companies involved with each project and say, "Let me develop a script and questions to ask the AI about what problems these companies have repeatedly had on previous projects."

If that happens and I encounter those challenges on the project, I can say, "Okay, you've had these problems. We're going to talk about that, because we don't want to repeat those mistakes on this project." Sadly, nine times out of ten, those making the mistakes don't learn from them. It could be because, as was the case with the Texas highway project, no one ever went back to them after a change order and informed them there was a mistake being repeated.

The ability to remove obstacles before they happen is priceless.

There's a famous architect in Europe who really is brilliant, with very out-of-the-box ideas. Repeatedly, that architect has run into major problems on their projects that have led to lawsuits. One almost bankrupted an entire city! Another included an interesting bridge with a glass floor, but the bridge ran over a river, and the glass got so slippery that people couldn't walk on it. They had to put rugs on it to make it useful -- defeating the purpose of the design. For a major city train station, part of the plan was a massive spinning concrete roof to open and close, which, by itself, would've cost about $200 million. The city had to go with a fixed roof and made other changes to cut down on the cost.

If you saw their work, you'd probably say, "We need to look at this architect for our project." However, after digging deeper into the past mistakes, you'd have to keep very close watch to ensure none of those mistakes were repeated. An AI database could show you those mistakes and warn you up front where that architect's creativity might have crossed the line --like I said, building inspectors can make exceptions, but Sir Isaac Newton can't be bribed.

Sometimes, several architects come to the table for large projects. If you can create an AI-enabled database on them, you can figure out their individual strengths and weaknesses and prepare to ask the right questions to make those judgments. The contract could make sure that this architect works on this portion where they're well experienced, and you could put another architect in a different section where they're stronger.

Continuing to collect data and adding it to the database as the project progresses might also point out mistakes that contractors are repeating. AI isn't designed to make decisions, and shouldn't, but it serves as a resource to provide data to support decisions. It could be a serious money saver.

## AI and Safety

We can always do better when it comes to safety. In 2001, New York City suffered a devastating act of terrorism resulting in the collapse of three World Trade Center buildings. No one knew exactly how many people were in those buildings, so nobody knew who was missing. It took weeks, and I don't know if we're actually sure we got every single person accounted for. Since then, in New York and other cities, buildings have collapsed because of fires or gas explosions. The question remains: did we account for everyone? In 2023, there were devastating fires on Maui in the Hawaiian Islands. At one point, I heard there were about 1,300 people unaccounted for, in addition to ninety-five known deaths spread over many square miles. Imagine trying to dig through all that to account for everyone.

Americans will never agree to be individually tagged in daily life; it would be too intrusive. Such tags have been used on construction sites, though, to help assess manpower and productivity. This could easily be adapted for greater functionality by allowing AI to sort through a lot of "background noise" during disasters or other events.

Construction site safety has come a long way, but this job still poses greater risks than most occupations. We no longer expect one death per mile or one death per million dollars of cost, as was common in previous generations. The adoption of this technology could further improve those numbers, and one major city has actually proposed expanding that very idea behind our manpower counting software to tag every person on every jobsite. They want to know where people are if a building collapses. What floor were they on? The last known location of any individual—worker, employee, or visitor—could mean the difference between a sigh of relief and a wake. That's the very best in actionable data—first responders could then search exactly where they know everybody was just moments ago.

Everything about One Team. Shared Success.sm is designed to create alignment, streamlining every facet of delivery. Tools that help us get there better and faster, make us better and faster. There is an entire use case in developing and managing our business processes with AI. From human resources, marketing and sales, risk, legal and compliance, product development, software engineering, supply chain and inventory management, and operations. AI is still a new technology, with its benefits and limitations still being explored. It has the potential to aid leaders in finding common ground on complex issues, fostering collaborative solutions that benefit everyone. I look forward to the benefits derived from its continual evolution.

# Conclusion

**"The best way to predict the future is to create it." (Abraham Lincoln)**

I said at the beginning that regardless of industry, projects--or deliverables or campaigns or sprints--of any kind follow a similar structure. There's a scope, a budget, a schedule, and a team that executes.

The CEO or the client will have a dream and assign you to create the plan and turn it into a reality. You'll engage other professionals to execute that plan. The completed project--in the case of construction, office buildings, hospitals, factories, bridges, tunnels, roads, etc.--will be used to function more efficiently, or create wealth for those who built it and others, to govern "We the People," and so on.

When the right people are in the right jobs, doing their best work, and proactively helping others improve, a team takes shape.

Such a team can perform miracles. In just twelve decades, we went from planes flying only 120 feet to around the world. We went from barely knowing what an electron was to a civilization that can't function without electronics. We went from a telephone, a catalog, and an encyclopedia to the World Wide Web on a phone in your pocket.

How? Teamwork.

Every project I described in this book, despite what you may have thought while reading, probably started out well intentioned. Somewhere along the way, the team fell apart. People started thinking more about themselves and their piece of the project than the project as a whole. They needed someone to reintroduce them to the benefits of collaboration and build--or rebuild--those individuals into a team. Once they saw what the team could do together, magical things happened.

All great advances disrupt cultures, and this new way of thinking disrupted the jobsite and the existing dynamics amongst team members--sometimes in uncomfortable ways. But everyone who bought into the new culture and the new model, at least enough to give it a try, became enthusiastic supporters. They left the confining box of conventional wisdom in the trash heap, and they profited; that data is proof alone that the process works.

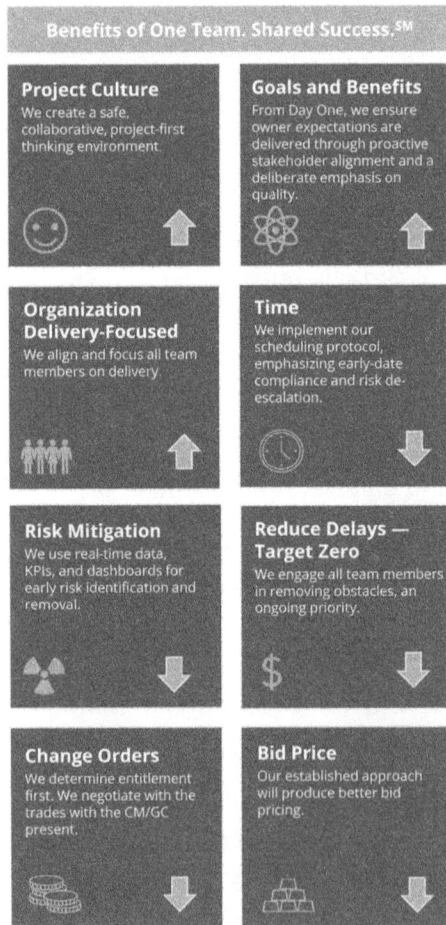

**Benefits of One Team. Shared Success.**<sup>SM</sup>

**Project Culture**
We create a safe, collaborative, project-first thinking environment.

**Goals and Benefits**
From Day One, we ensure owner expectations are delivered through proactive stakeholder alignment and a deliberate emphasis on quality.

**Organization Delivery-Focused**
We align and focus all team members on delivery.

**Time**
We implement our scheduling protocol, emphasizing early-date compliance and risk de-escalation.

**Risk Mitigation**
We use real-time data, KPIs, and dashboards for early risk identification and removal.

**Reduce Delays — Target Zero**
We engage all team members in removing obstacles, an ongoing priority.

**Change Orders**
We determine entitlement first. We negotiate with the trades with the CM/GC present.

**Bid Price**
Our established approach will produce better bid pricing.

Effective teamwork is rooted in establishing a collaborative culture that prioritizes project goals from the start. Aligning all team members enhances effectiveness and focuses on quality, ensuring timely project delivery. Utilizing real-time data for risk mitigation, actively engaging team members to overcome obstacles, and strategically handling change orders and bid pricing further streamline processes. These combined efforts reduce or eliminate delays and costs, leading to competitive pricing and significantly improved project outcomes.

I have always resisted fitting into any predefined categories. I find that I'm happiest and most productive when I'm not boxed in. When I'm confined, I'm unhappy and don't do my best work, nor does anyone else I've ever known.

I didn't think about it in those terms when I was younger. I wasn't worried about doing my best work, let alone what that looked like. They told me I was difficult throughout high school and for most of my young adult life, and if you knew me then, you would probably agree.

As I grew as a professional, I still never deliberately thought, "I'm going to change the way people work together, especially in the built environment." I developed a disruptive mindset habitually, because I could see an easier way to do things, and my teams made them work. So when I was recognized as a Fifty Over 50 "Age Disruptor" in New York by The City & State NY, it clicked: some things needed to be disrupted, and look at all that has taken place because they were.

Success or failure, it's all about your team.

I'm betting on your success.

# IT'S ALL ABOUT YOUR TEAM

## CRITICAL TASK CHECKLIST
## FOR PROJECT EXECUTION

Your projects deserve the best. This checklist aims to ensure that your project management approach adheres to the "One Team. Shared Success.$^{SM}$" philosophy, boosts efficiency, strengthens partnerships, and drives outstanding project results.

Every task on this checklist is crafted to proactively address possible issues, promoting seamless execution and coordination among all stakeholders. Modifications may be needed based on specific project contexts and environments.

### Scan here to grab your
### Checklist for Project Execution.

www.grouppmx.com/its-all-about-your-team